METAPHOR
AND SYMBOL

Special Issue:
Metaphor and Artificial Intelligence
John A. Barnden and Mark G. Lee, Guest Editors

Routledge
Taylor & Francis Group

LONDON AND NEW YORK

This journal is abstracted or indexed in *ISI: Current Contents/Social & Behavioral Sciences, Social Sciences Citation Index, Research Alert, Social SciSearch; Linguistic Abstracts; Linguistics and Language Behavior Abstracts; MLA Directory of Periodicals; MLA International Bibliography; PsycINFO/Psychological Abstracts; Sociological Abstracts.* Microform copies of this journal are available through Bell & Howell Information and Learning, P.O. Box 1346, Ann Arbor, MI 48106-1346.

First published 2001 by Lawrence Erlbaum Associates, Inc.

2 Park Square, Milton Park, Abingdon, Oxfordshire OX14 4RN
52 Vanderbilt Avenue, New York, NY 10017

Routledge is an imprint of the Taylor & Francis Group, an informa business

First issued in paperback 2019

ISBN 13: 978-0-8058-9730-2 (pbk)
ISSN 1092-6488

Cover: William Blake's *Ancient of Days* is reproduced with the kind permission of the Whitworth Art Gallery, University of Manchester, England.

METAPHOR
AND SYMBOL

Volume 16, Numbers 1 & 2

Special Issue:
Metaphor and Artificial Intelligence
John A. Barnden and Mark G. Lee, Guest Editors

METAPHOR AND SYMBOL, 16(1&2), 1–3
Copyright © 2001, Lawrence Erlbaum Associates, Inc.

Introduction to the Special Issue on Metaphor and Artificial Intelligence

John A. Barnden and Mark G. Lee

School of Computer Science
University of Birmingham

This special issue arose out of contributions at a symposium on metaphor, artificial intelligence (AI), and cognition held as part of the 1999 Convention of the Society for the Study of Artificial Intelligence and the Simulation of Behaviour in Edinburgh, Scotland. The articles in this issue have in most cases undergone major revision as a result both of interactions at the symposium and of the journal's peer reviewing process.

The main orientation of the symposium was toward computational models and psychological processing models of metaphorical understanding. This orientation is well reflected in the selection of articles in this special issue. Two are about implemented computational systems for handling different aspects of metaphor understanding. One of these articles is by Thomas and Mareschal (2001/this issue) and the other is by ourselves (Lee & Barnden, 2001/this issue). They contrast in many respects, one of which is that the former is within the connectionist paradigm, whereas the latter is in the traditional symbolic paradigm. Two of the remaining articles, those by van Genabith (2001/this issue) and by Vogel (2001/this issue), are largely about how metaphor can be accommodated in accepted logical representational frameworks. They therefore help to show that handling metaphor computationally is not something that need require revolutions in current practice in AI or formal semantics. Three articles are, in different ways, on psychological processes involved in metaphor understanding. These are by Dortfeld and McGlone (2001/this issue); Brisard, Frisson, and Sandra (2001/this issue); and Noveck, Bianco, and Castry (2001/this issue). The first recommends that currently competing processing models in psychology could cooperate and complement each other rather than compete. The second provides evidence in favor of meta-

Requests for reprints should be sent to John A. Barnden, School of Computer Science, University of Birmingham, Edgbaston, Birmingham B15 2TT, England. E-mail: J.A.Barnden@cs.bham.ac.uk

phorical processing taking more time than literal processing when timings are taken within sentences, not just at the end of sentences. The third, relatedly, points to evidence that metaphorical processing comes with extra cost, but that the cost brings additional benefits. Finally, we include one article, by Neumann (2001/this issue), that is distinctly different in flavor from the others, as it is a detailed linguistic study, using data from German and Japanese, underpinning the cross-linguistic cognitive reality of conceptual metaphors.

The symposium proceedings (*Proceedings of the AISB'99 Symposium on Metaphor, Artificial Intelligence, and Cognition,* 1999) contains further papers of various types, including experimental psychological results, results of linguistic analysis of examples and linguistic corpora, observations on metaphor in art and architectural design, and steps toward the handling of metaphor in machine translation of languages. Abstracts are available at http://www.cs.bham.ac.uk/~jab/AISB-99.

From our own point of view as AI researchers into metaphor, we find it valuable to take part in interdisciplinary forums, and we hope that our authors from other disciplines do so too. We were touched by the extent to which various symposium participants from outside AI were surprised at the very existence of AI researchers interested in a subject such as metaphor. Undoubtedly, metaphor is currently a minority concern within AI (although it should be pointed out that the minority has been in place since early in the development of AI). However, we believe that there is new room to hope for growth of interest in the subject within AI. The readers of this journal probably do not need to be convinced of the prevalence and centrality of metaphor in everyday text and speech. Because technological developments are making it increasingly possible and important to include AI elements in publicly available or commercial software, and natural language processing is an important aspect of user friendliness, issues such as metaphor are increasingly becoming looming practical obstacles as opposed to pies in the distant sky. In particular, the development of large text and speech corpora and of tools capable of dealing with their immense size make it reasonable to embark on developing methods for the large-scale semiautomated analysis of metaphor in real discourse.

In many areas of AI, not least language processing, AI research and psychological research must interact for two rather different reasons. One is the more obvious one and is often pointed out: Studies of how the human mind operates could suggest mechanisms to AI system developers, and conversely, the detailed computational or formal modeling that AI researchers do (whether they have connectionist, symbolic, or other orientations) can contribute to psychological theorizing—it can suggest rich computational difficulties, abilities, subtleties, compromises, hybrids, and other possibilities. The second, less often considered reason is that if an AI system is to interact with people, notably by language, it must to some extent appreciate the mental states and processes of those people. For example, an AI system that understands metaphorical language—everyday language—must have some appreciation of how the speakers or writers expect or intend it to be understood. Psychology can throw light on such expectations and intentions and is therefore relevant to the development of the AI system, even if the system itself is not intended to be a psychological model. Of course, the extent to which the system must be able to appreciate the workings of people's minds need be no greater than the extent to which we as ordinary language understanders can do it, and that extent is often small enough.

The articles in this special issue were selected by the journal's standard mechanisms of blind peer review. This applied just as much to our own article as to others. We are grateful to our small band of reviewers, especially Albert Katz, for their immensely hard work; to *Metaphor & Symbol* for its receptiveness, patience, general guidance, and careful attention to the content and style of the articles; to all the other authors of the included articles for their hard work and their interest in contributing to the symposium and special issue; and to authors whose articles we were unable to include, but who nevertheless made a valuable contribution to the symposium and enlarged our own knowledge of metaphor.

REFERENCES

Bortfeld, H., & McGlone, M. S. (2001/this issue). The continuum of metaphor processing. *Metaphor and Symbol, 16*, 75–86.

Brisard, F., Frisson, S., & Sandra, D. (2001/this issue). Processing unfamiliar metaphors in a self-paced reading task. *Metaphor and Symbol, 16*, 87–108.

Lee, M. G., & Barnden, J. A. (2001/this issue). Reasoning about mixed metaphors within an implemented artificial intelligence system. *Metaphor and Symbol, 16*, 29–42.

Neumann, C. (2001/this issue). Is metaphor universal? Cross-language evidence from German and Japanese. *Metaphor and Symbol, 16*, 123–142.

Noveck, I. A., Bianco, M., & Castry, A. (2001/this issue). The costs and benefits of metaphor. *Metaphor and Symbol, 16*, 109–121.

Proceedings of the AISB'99 Symposium on Metaphor, Artificial Intelligence, and Cognition. (1999). Brighton, England: University of Sussex, Society for the Study of Artificial Intelligence and the Simulation of Behaviour.

Thomas, M. S. C., & Mareschal, D. (2001/this issue). Metaphor as categorization: A connectionist implementation. *Metaphor and Symbol, 16*, 5–27.

van Genabith, J. (2001/this issue). Metaphors, logic, and type theory. *Metaphor and Symbol, 16*, 43–57.

Vogel, C. (2001/this issue). Dynamic semantics for metaphor. *Metaphor and Symbol, 16*, 59–74.

METAPHOR AND SYMBOL, *16*(1&2), 5–27
Copyright © 2001, Lawrence Erlbaum Associates, Inc.

Metaphor as Categorization: A Connectionist Implementation

Michael S. C. Thomas

Neurocognitive Development Unit
Institute of Child Health

Denis Mareschal

Centre for Brain and Cognitive Development
School of Psychology
Birkbeck College

A key issue for models of metaphor comprehension is to explain how, in some metaphorical comparison *"A is B,"* only some features of B are transferred to A. The features of B that are transferred to A depend both on A and on B. This is the central thrust of Black's (1979) well-known interaction theory of metaphor comprehension. However, this theory is somewhat abstract, and it is not obvious how it may be implemented in terms of mental representations and processes. In this article, we describe a simple computational model of online metaphor comprehension that combines Black's interaction theory with the idea that metaphor comprehension is a type of categorization process (Glucksberg & Keysar, 1990, 1993). The model is based on a distributed connectionist network depicting semantic memory (McClelland & Rumelhart, 1986). The network learns feature-based information about various concepts. A metaphor is comprehended by applying a representation of the first term (A) to the network storing knowledge of the second term (B), in an attempt to categorize it as an exemplar of B. The output of this network is a representation of A transformed by the knowledge of B. We explain how this process embodies an interaction of knowledge between the 2 terms of the metaphor, how it accords with the contemporary theory of metaphor stating that comprehension for literal and metaphorical comparisons is carried out by identical mechanisms (Gibbs, 1994), and how it accounts for existing empirical evidence (Glucksberg, McGlone, & Manfredi, 1997) and generates

Requests for reprints should be sent to Michael S. C. Thomas, Neurocognitive Development Unit, Institute of Child Health, 30, Guilford Street, London WC1N 1EH, England. E-mail: M.Thomas@ich.ucl.ac.uk

new predictions. In this model, the distinction between literal and metaphorical language is one of degree, not of kind.

Why use metaphor in language? Gibbs (1994) summarized three kinds of answers to this question (Fainsilber & Ortony, 1987; Ortony, 1975). First, the *inexpressibility hypothesis* suggests that metaphors allow us to express ideas that we cannot easily express using literal language. Second, the *compactness hypothesis* suggests that metaphors allow the communication of complex configurations of information to capture the richness of a particular experience. The use of literal language to communicate the same meaning would be cumbersome and inefficient. Third, the *vividness hypothesis* suggests that the ideas communicable via a metaphor are in fact richer than those we may achieve using literal language.

When we receive information coded in the form of a metaphor (e.g., not that Richard is brave, aggressive, etc., but that *"Richard is a lion"*), how do we process such language to extract its vivid meaning? The traditional view in philosophy and linguistics was that language comprehension and production are built around literal language, that metaphorical language is both harder to comprehend (given that it is literally false; in our example, Richard is not a lion) and requires special processing mechanisms to decode. Although it is distinguished by its communicative advantages, metaphor was seen as a purely linguistic phenomenon (Grice, 1975; Searle, 1975). More recently, this view has been challenged on two grounds (e.g., Gibbs, 1994, 1996; Lakoff, 1993). First, it is claimed that metaphor is conceptual rather than linguistic. Second, it is claimed that metaphor is not an add-on to the more primary literal language processing system, but a key aspect of language itself, sharing the same kind of processing mechanisms. In this article, we focus on the second of these claims.

The argument that metaphor comprehension does not require special processing mechanisms has two strands (Gibbs & Gerrig, 1989). The first is that online processing studies suggest that (with appropriate contextual support) metaphors and literal statements take the same amount of time to process (e.g., Inhoff, Lima, & Carroll, 1984; Ortony, Schallert, Reynolds, & Antos, 1978). This seems to rule out the possibility that metaphors are initially processed as literal statements, found to be false, and only then processed by metaphor-specific mechanisms. It does not, however, rule out the possibility that literal and metaphorical meanings of a sentence may be computed simultaneously and in parallel by separate mechanisms. The second strand suggests that literal language processing is no easier than metaphorical processing, given that both rely on a common ground between speaker and listener to comprehend what a given utterance means (Gibbs, 1994). That is, an apparently literal statement may well have an implicated meaning given a certain set of shared assumptions between speaker and listener. If both types of language involve similar problems, it makes sense to see them as engaging the same sort of mechanisms.

Black (1955, 1962, 1979) outlined three views of how the metaphor comprehension process may work. In the first of these, the substitution view, to understand the metaphorical comparison *"Richard is a lion,"* this comparison must initially be replaced by a set of literal propositions that fit the same context (e.g., Richard is brave, Richard is aggressive). In the comparison view, the metaphor is taken to imply that the two terms are similar to each other in certain (communicatively relevant) respects. For example, both Richard and the lion are brave, aggressive, and so forth. The intention of the comparison is to highlight these properties in the first term *Richard.* In effect, the comparison is shorthand for the simile *"Richard is like a lion."* In the interactive view, the comparison of the two terms in the metaphor is not taken to emphasize preexisting similarities between them, but itself plays a role in creating that similarity. The topic (first term) and vehicle (second term) interact such that the topic itself causes the selection of certain of the features of the vehicle, which may then be used in the comparison with the topic. In turn, this parallel implication complex may cause changes in our understanding of the vehicle in the comparison.

Although the interaction view has been described as "the dominant theory in the multidisciplinary study of metaphor" (Gibbs, 1994, p. 234), it has nevertheless been criticized for the vagueness of its central terms. One of the key issues for psycholinguistic models of metaphor comprehension is explanation of the nature of the interaction between topic and vehicle that constrains the emergent meaning of the comparison. Three main models have been proposed. These are the salience imbalance model (Ortony, 1979, 1993), the structural mapping model (Gentner, 1983; Gentner & Clements, 1988), and the class inclusion model (Glucksberg & Keysar, 1990, 1993). The *salience imbalance model* proposes that metaphors are similarity statements with two terms that share attributes. However, the salience of these attributes is much higher in the second term than the first. The comparison serves to emphasize these attributes in the first term. The *structural mapping model* suggests that topic and vehicle can be matched in three ways: in terms of their relational structure (i.e., in the hierarchical organization of their properties and attributes), in terms of those properties themselves, or in terms of both relational structure and properties. People tend to show a preference for relational mappings in metaphors. The *class inclusion model* proposes that metaphors are understood as categorical assertions. In a metaphor *"A is B,"* A is assigned to a category denoted by B (i.e., Richard falls into the class of brave, aggressive things, of which a lion is a prototypical member). Only those categories of which B is a member that could also plausibly contain A are considered as the intended meaning of the categorical assertion.

The view of metaphor as a form of categorization seems perhaps most consistent with the claim that metaphor comprehension requires no special processes over and above literal comprehension. Both the salience imbalance model and the structural mapping model imply a property-matching procedure that is engaged for nonliteral comparisons (Glucksberg, McGlone, & Manfredi, 1997). Moreover, Glucksberg et al. (1997) argued that the class inclusion theory is empirically distinguishable from these property-matching models. Although literal comparisons are asymmetric (in that the similarity of two terms can be rated differently depending on the order of presentation; e.g., Tversky & Gati, 1982), class inclusion statements should be more than asymmetric; they should be nonreversible. *"The lion is Richard"* should make very much less sense than *"Richard is a lion,"* unless Richard happens to be a prototypical member of a category of which lion could also be a member. Second, Glucksberg et al. claimed that the topic and vehicle should make very different (although interactive) contributions to the metaphor's meaning, and that these contributions are predictable. The vehicle provides the properties that may be attributed to the topic, but the listener's familiarity with the topic constrains those properties that may be attributed to it. Glucksberg et al. primed comprehension of metaphorical comparisons by preexposure to either topic or vehicle. They predicted that only comparisons involving topics with few potentially relevant attributes, or vehicles with few properties available as candidate attributes, should benefit from preexposure. In their view, neither property-matching model should predict the nonreversibility or specific interactivity effects. Nevertheless, Glucksberg et al. found empirical support for both of their predictions.

The class inclusion model contrasts with Lakoff and colleagues' theory that metaphors rely on established mappings between pairs of domains in long-term memory (Lakoff, 1987, 1990, 1993; Lakoff & Johnson, 1980; Lakoff & Turner, 1989). Thus, comprehension of the metaphor *"this relationship is going nowhere"* proceeds via a preexisting system of correspondences between the conceptual domains of *love* and *journey*. The class inclusion theory, on the other hand, posits no such preexisting metaphorical structures. In a comparison of the class inclusion and conceptual metaphor theories, McGlone (1996) determined that it was not yet possible to find conclusive evidence for either theory. McGlone presented four experiments, employing metaphor paraphrasing, comparison, and cued recall, the results of which he took to support the class inclusion theory over the conceptual metaphor theory. However, he admitted that the use of these offline measures may not have tapped the use of conceptual metaphors during online interpretation. Evidence for the class inclusion model comes from the irreversibility of metaphors and related discourse phenomena (Glucksberg, 1991), whereas the primary evidence for the conceptual metaphor theory comes from the observed systematicity of idiomatic expressions in certain semantic domains. Lakoff (1993) criticized the class inclusion model for its use of metaphorical attributive categories to mediate metaphor comprehension. Thus, the metaphor *"my job is a jail"* must be understood via appeal to the category of restraining things (of which jail is a prototypical member). However, the application of the term *restraining* to the concept *job* is itself metaphorical. Yet Lakoff's (1993) own theory incurs the same problem in his use of the invariance principle, by which domains are linked in long-term memory. Thus, the domains of *containers* and *cate-*

gories, for instance, are linked in a particular way such that "source domain interiors correspond to target domain interiors" (p. 215). However, the notion of the *interior* of a container can only be metaphorically applied to the concept *category*. In sum, it is premature to reject either of these theories at the current time. In what follows, we concentrate on the class inclusion theory.

In this article, our aim is to propose a computational model of metaphor comprehension based on a categorization device, as opposed to the property-matching device that would have to lie at the heart of a salience imbalance or a structural mapping model. Because our model is based on a previously proposed mechanism of semantic memory, it exemplifies the idea that metaphor comprehension is not a special function of the language processing system. Indeed, we suggest that within this mechanism, literal and metaphorical comparisons are distinguished only quantitatively, not qualitatively. The implemented model demonstrates in concrete terms how topic and vehicle interact in metaphor comprehension, addressing some of the vagueness in the interaction position. Finally, we show how the model accounts for both of the empirical findings demonstrated by Glucksberg et al. (1997) and how it generates new predictions.

First, however, we lay out the assumptions of the metaphor by pattern completion (MPC) model.

ASSUMPTIONS OF THE MODEL

The model builds on the following assumptions:

1. The aim of comprehension is the ongoing development of a semantic representation, and that representation is feature based.

2. The ongoing semantic representation is continually monitored against expectations based on a common ground between listener and speaker. Specifically with regard to metaphor comprehension, the ongoing semantic representation is monitored for degree of expected meaning change. (It will be monitored in other ways for other nonliteral communication.)

3. Comparisons of the form *"A is B"* are class inclusion statements where the intended meaning is that A is a member of category B and so should inherit its attributes (Glucksberg & Keysar, 1990, 1993).

4. The meaning produced by a metaphor is the result of using a categorization mechanism to transfer attributes from B to A when A is not in fact a member of B. However, membership of B is not all or nothing, but depends on degree of featural overlap.

5. The categorization mechanism is an autoassociative neural network. Category membership is established by the accuracy of reproduction of a novel input A to a network trained to reproduce exemplars of category B. The output of such a network is a version of A transformed to make it more consistent with B.

6. Metaphorical comparisons must exceed some expected level of semantic distortion (for a given context) to be interpreted as metaphorical. When a comparison is interpreted as metaphorical, not all feature changes induced in the topic A are accepted as the communicative intent of the comparison. More specifically, the accepted features of the comparison are those initially nonzero features of the topic A that are amplified by the transformation caused by the vehicle knowledge base B.

7. Metaphorical mappings caused by the topic may be learned in the network storing the vehicle knowledge. The topic may become a (highly atypical) member of the vehicle category, so changing that category in long-term memory. Thus, metaphors may either be computed online or retrieved from long-term memory.

Before describing the details of the model, we wish to expand on two of these assumptions and situate our model with respect to previous connectionist models of metaphor comprehension. The first is the idea that meaning can be described as a set of features, or in connectionist terms, as a vector representation. Although there is a significant debate surrounding the legitimacy of feature vectors, much research has used vector-based semantic representations. For instance, connectionist models of word recognition that employ such representations have successfully captured a great deal of empirical data in both normal and impaired language processing (Plaut, McClelland, Seidenberg, & Patterson, 1996; Plaut & Shallice, 1993). Moreover, using a semantic priming paradigm, McRae, Cree, and McNorgan (1998) generated empirical predictions for the feature-based theory of lexical semantic representation and its main competitor, the hierarchical semantic network theory. Their results supported feature-based accounts, finding no evidence that priming proceeded via intervening superordinate nodes rather than shared feature sets. McRae et al. concluded that "lexical concepts are not represented as static nodes in a hierarchical system" (p. 681). Finally, corpus-based approaches have demonstrated that valid measures of word meaning can be generated using vector-based cooccurrence statistics of the context in which words appear (Lund & Burgess, 1996). This has led to new theories of the acquisition of word meaning per se (Landauer & Dumais, 1997). Although there are certainly problems with vector-based accounts and their difficulty in representing conceptual structure, they are nevertheless an active theoretical approach to the representation of meaning.

The second assumption is that connectionist networks are a valid cognitive model of categorization. Connectionist models have tended to take two approaches to categorization (see, e.g., Small, Hart, Nguyen, & Gordon, 1996). In one approach, the network takes object features as inputs and maps to category names as outputs. In the other, a network is trained simply to reproduce the object features for the category it is storing (a task known as autoassociation). Category membership is tested depending on the accuracy with which a novel input is reproduced. An accurate reproduction indicates a high probability of category membership. It is the latter approach we adopt for our model. This approach has been used previously in models of the acquisition of word meaning (Plunkett, Sinha, Mueller, & Strandsby, 1992) and of semantic memory (McClelland & Rumelhart, 1986; Small et al., 1996).

A number of previous researchers have exploited the soft multiple constraint satisfaction capabilities of connectionist systems to propose models that find systematic mappings between the two concepts of a metaphor. Some of these models build in complex preexisting structure to represent the various concepts (e.g., Holyoak & Thagard, 1989; Hummel & Holyoak, 1997; Narayanan, 1999; Veale & Keane, 1992; Weber, 1994). Others have emphasized featural representations. Thus, Sun (1995) showed how a network trained on a subset of metaphors relating items in the landscape to facial features (around the core metaphor *"billboards are warts"*) could generalize this knowledge to produce plausible meanings for metaphors it had not seen (see also Chandler, 1991). In our model we minimize the weight attributed to structural relations in metaphor, focusing on the learnability of the concepts in a distributed system. Models that build in complex preexisting structured representations entrust much of their performance to the precise nature of these representations, limiting their generality and robustness. We build in no a priori metaphor structures other than the ability of a system to select the knowledge with which it attempts to categorize a given input. However, the concepts learned by our model do contain structure in the form of systematic (although probabilistic) covariation of the features that define them.

THE MPC MODEL

The model we present is simple and is primarily intended to illustrate the metaphor as categorization approach. Figure 1 demonstrates the model architecture. A three-layer connectionist network is trained to autoassociate (reproduce across the output units) semantic vector representations of exemplars from a number of different categories. Each category knowledge base is stored across a different set of hidden units.[1] Metaphor processing is modeled by inputting a semantic vector for the topic to the part of the network storing a category of which it is not a member (i.e., the vehicle). The output of the network is a semantic representation of the topic transformed to make it more consistent with the vehicle. To understand why this transformation should occur, we need to consider a property of connectionist networks known as *pattern completion*.

Pattern completion is a property of connectionist networks that derives from their nonlinear processing (Rumelhart & McClelland, 1986). A network trained to

---

[1]The use of separate banks of hidden units is not a necessary assumption of the model. "Soft" modularity of knowledge bases can be achieved by using input and output labels to index each concept during training and categorization.

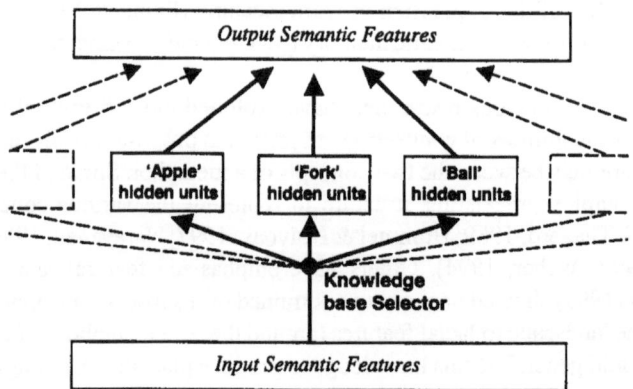

FIGURE 1   Architecture of the metaphor by pattern completion model.

respond to a given input set will still respond adequately given noisy versions of the input patterns. For example, if an autoassociator is trained to reproduce the vector <0 1 0 0> and is subsequently given the input <.2 .6 .2 .2>, its output is likely to be much closer to the vector it "knows," perhaps <.0 .9 .0 .0>. An input is transformed to make it more consistent with the knowledge that the network has been previously trained on. The connection weights store the feature correlation information in previously experienced examples. If a partial input is presented to the network, it can use that correlation information to reconstruct the missing features.

When processing metaphors, the input is not a noisy version of a pattern on which the network has previously been trained, but an exemplar of another concept. The output is then a transformed version of the topic, changed to make it more consistent with the knowledge stored about the vehicle. Metaphorical meaning emerges as a result of deliberate misclassification. As shown shortly, the way in which a network transforms an input depends on that input. In this way, the model captures the interactivity between the terms of the metaphor.

For this simple model, we chose a small set of features with which to describe the concepts. To generate knowledge bases for separate concepts, the network was trained to autoassociate exemplars of each concept. For simplicity, we restricted the model to the formation of *"A is B"* metaphors between three concepts: apples, balls, and forks. Two of these could plausibly be used in a metaphorical comparison (e.g., *"the apple is a ball"*), one of them much less so (e.g., *"the apple is a fork"*).

The concepts were defined by a set of prototypical tokens representing different kinds of apples, balls, and forks that could be encountered in the individual's world (see Table 1). The network was not trained on the prototypes themselves, but on exemplars clustered around these prototypes. Exemplars were generated from each prototype by adding Gaussian noise (variance = 0.15) to the original.

TABLE 1
Prototype Feature Sets for Each Category

	Color				Actions		Shape			Texture		Size	
Concepts	Red	Green	Brown	White	Edible	Thrown	Round	Irregular	Pointed	Soft	Hard	Handsized	Lapsized
Apples													
Red	1	0	0	0	1	.2	.8	.3	0	.3	.7	1	0
Green	0	1	0	0	1	.2	.8	.3	0	.3	.7	1	0
Rotten	0	0	1	0	0	.2	.8	.3	0	1	0	1	0
Balls													
Baseballs	0	0	0	1	0	1	1	0	0	0	1	.9	.1
Beach balls													
Red	1	0	0	0	0	1	1	0	0	1	0	.1	.9
Green	0	1	0	0	0	1	1	0	0	1	0	.1	.9
Forks													
Fork	0	0	0	.9	0	.1	0	0	1	0	1	.7	.3

The exemplars for each concept formed three training sets used to develop the network's three prior knowledge bases about apples, balls, and forks. The existence of a prior knowledge base is a necessary feature of metaphor comprehension. Prior knowledge bases are analogous to Black's (1979) implicative complex and reflect an individual's personal experience with exemplars of each concept. The apple subnetwork was trained to autoassociate patterns corresponding to 10 exemplars of each of three apple kinds (e.g., red, green, and rotten) for a total of 30 patterns. Similarly, the ball subnetwork was trained to autoassociate 10 exemplars of three different kinds, for a total of 30 patterns. Finally, the fork subnetwork was trained to autoassociate 10 exemplars of one kind, for a total of 10 patterns. Because there was only one kind of fork (as opposed to three kinds of both apples and balls), a single blank training pattern (zero input and output) was added to the fork training set to inhibit overlearning of the fork exemplars. All networks were trained with backpropagation using the following parameter values: learning rate = 0.1, momentum = 0.0, initial weight range = ±0.5. Each subnetwork (knowledge base) was trained for 1,000 epochs. All reported results are averaged over $n = 10$ replications using different random starting weights and concept exemplars.

After training, the network demonstrated prototype effects in each knowledge base. They responded most strongly to the prototypes for each category, despite never encountering them in training (cf. human performance; Posner & Keele, 1968). This suggests that the apple, ball, and fork categories had been adequately learned. Metaphors were processed by the redirection of information flow into one knowledge base or another. The role of the *is* in the *"A is B"* metaphor is to trigger that redirection.

RESULTS

Interaction Between Topic and Vehicle

Figure 2 shows the transformation of the semantic features of an apple concept for the metaphor *"the apple is a ball."* The input is an exemplar of apple close to its prototype kind and is presented to the network storing knowledge about balls. The effect of this metaphor is to produce as output a representation of apple in which the suitability for throwing, the hardness, and roundness features are exaggerated; the edibility feature is reduced; and the color features become more ambiguous. Provided the context-dependent threshold for semantic distortion is exceeded, this metaphor will be interpreted to mean that the apple in question is round, hard, and likely to be thrown.

In Glucksberg and Keysar's (1990) class inclusion theory, a metaphor highlights an underlying category of which both topic and vehicle are members (but the vehicle is the prototypical member). Thus, *"my job is a jail"* highlights that job is a member of the underlying category (restraining things). In the MPC model, one

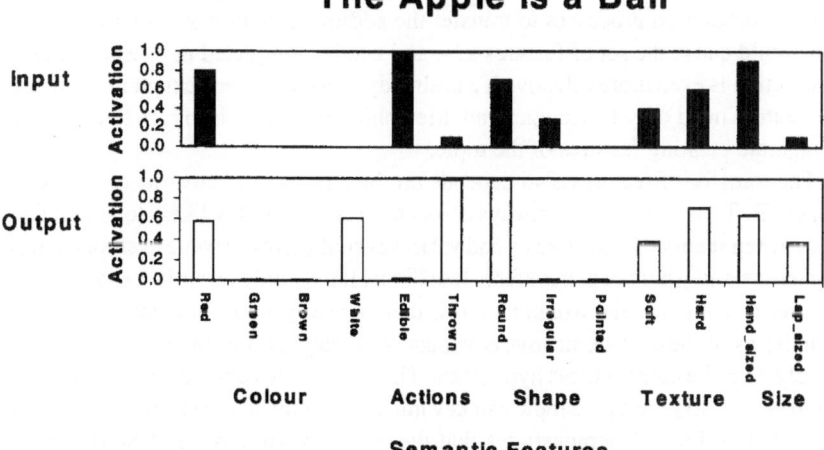

FIGURE 2   Transformations of semantic features by a metaphorical comparison (topic/input = apple; vehicle/network = ball).

could see such a new inclusive category as emerging from the juxtaposition. That is, the features of A that are emphasized by processing in the B network define the category of which apple and ball are both members (but of which ball is the prototypical member): hard round things that can be thrown. This is a possible response to Lakoff's (1993) criticism that in the class inclusion theory, metaphor comprehension relies on unlikely preexisting metaphoric attributive categories (e.g., restraining things in the preceding example). In the model presented here, such attributive categories are newly created by the categorization process itself.

Alternatively, we could describe this transformation in terms of Black's (1979) parallel implication complex. Either way, these modified features are a result of the interaction of the topic and vehicle. For example, note that despite the fact that 20 of the 30 ball exemplars are soft beach balls, apple is still made to look harder rather than softer by this metaphor. This is because the apple is closer in size to a hard baseball than it is to a soft beach ball. The semantic transformation is not a default imposition of ball features onto those of an apple, but an interaction between stored ball knowledge and the nature of the apple exemplar being presented to the ball subnetwork. Thus, the model offers an instantiation of Black's interactive theory of metaphor comprehension.

We can now attempt to formulate a clearer answer to the question of why in a metaphor *"A is B,"* some features of B should be transferred to A but not others. Let us assume that features x, y, and z tend to co-occur in exemplars of B. Transfer of feature z from B to A will occur only when features x and y are present in A.

Concept A can "key in" to a strong covariance of features in B, thus triggering the pattern completion processes to transfer the additional feature z. Pattern completion would cause the set of features x, y, and z to be completed in A. Such pattern completion is even more effective if z is already present to some extent in A, so that this feature need only be exaggerated. Metaphorical comparisons are thus used to exaggerate existing features of the topic.

The transfer of features also depends on the strictness of covariance in exemplars of B. Thus, if x, y, and z always co-occur in B, A is highly likely to inherit feature z when it already possesses x and y. However, if there are some exemplars of B that have x and y but not z, transfer is less likely. It may only occur if A shares other features of the particular exemplars of B that have x, y, and z in common.

In terms of the communicative advantage of metaphor, this model accords most closely with the compactness hypothesis. That is, vehicles embody a covariance of features that, so long as the topic can key into them, may be transferred to the topic as a whole. Figure 2 demonstrates that the transformation of the features of the topic is a subtle one: Features are not all or nothing, but enhanced or attenuated. It may also be that subtle transformations of meaning of this sort cannot be achieved by the use of literal language alone. Thus, the model may also accord with the inexpressibility hypothesis.

The Reversibility of Metaphors

Glucksberg et al. (1997) claimed that metaphors are characterized by the property of nonreversibility, a property that only the class inclusion model can explain. The authors had participants rate the sense of literal and metaphorical comparisons in original ("sermons are sleeping pills") and reversed ("sleeping pills are sermons") formats. The participants also paraphrased the two versions. The experimenters judged the forward and reverse paraphrases for how much sense they made. The results showed that literal comparisons were far more reversible than metaphors. Glucksberg et al. concluded that their data "provided strong support for the claim that metaphors and similes either lose or change meaning when reversed" (p. 57).

Figure 3 shows the transformation for the metaphor "the ball is an apple," the reverse of the metaphor shown in Figure 2. In Figure 3, the effect of comparing the ball to an apple is to exaggerate the softness and irregularity and edibility of the ball, reducing its likelihood of being thrown, its size, and its roundness. The semantic effect of this metaphor is quite different from that in the previous case, despite the fact that the feature overlap of ball exemplars and apple exemplars defining the knowledge bases is the same in each case. The change in meaning between the forward and reverse metaphors, found in the empirical data, arises in the MPC model from the nonlinear nature of its transformations. These transformations are not symmetrical.

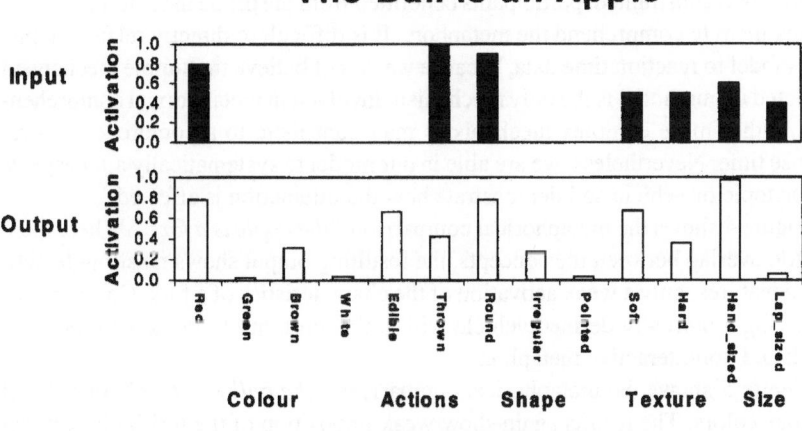

FIGURE 3   The nonreversibility of metaphorical comparisons.

Glucksberg et al. (1997) noted that literal similarity statements are asymmetric—the rated similarity changes with the order of presentation of two terms—and that property-matching models can account for this asymmetry by rating properties of the first and second term differently. However, Glucksberg et al. maintained that nonreversibility is different in kind than asymmetry, and that property-matching models such as the salience imbalance model and the structural mapping model cannot account for nonreversibility. We see literal and metaphorical comparisons as lying on a continuum, just as category membership can be a graded rather than binary phenomenon. We have shown elsewhere that an architecture similar to the MPC model is able to account for the asymmetry in general similarity judgments (Thomas & Mareschal, 1997). Reversibility and asymmetry are also matters of degree. Support for this is provided by Sternberg, Tourangeau, and Nigro (1979), who found an inverse relation between the similarity of two terms in a comparison and the aesthetic impact of that comparison. Metaphors are about having just the right amount of dissimilarity. The greater the dissimilarity, the greater the asymmetry.

Predictability of Interactions

Glucksberg et al. (1997) manipulated the ambiguity of vehicles and the number of potentially relevant attributes of topics in metaphorical comparisons. They primed comprehension of metaphors by prior exposure of either the topic or the vehicle. The results showed that when either ambiguity or number of potentially relevant attributes was constrained, participants benefitted from the prime in terms of the time it took them to comprehend the metaphors. It is difficult to directly relate our current model to reaction time data, because we do not believe the simple mechanism depicted in our model is the only mechanism involved in metaphorical comprehension. Other more complex mechanisms may contribute to a comprehension response time. Nevertheless, we are able in our model to systematically alter aspects of the topic or vehicle and demonstrate how the interaction is affected.

Figure 4 shows the metaphorical comparison *"the apple is a fork."* Where there is little overlap between the concepts, the resulting output shows no strongly activated features, only a weak activation of the characteristics of a fork. Comparisons involving a narrowly defined vehicle with little similarity to the topic produce a weak and noninteractive metaphor.

Figure 5 shows the metaphorical comparison *"the ball is a fork"* for balls of various colors. The results again show weak imposition of the fork's characteristics, except when the ball is the same color as the fork. In this case, the topic can key into the narrowly defined vehicle concept and evoke a stronger transformation.

Figure 6 shows the metaphorical comparison *"the ball is an apple,"* again for balls of various colors. Here the vehicle, apple, is more ambiguous than fork, in that it has more widely varying prototypes. The resulting transformation is thus more interactive; that is, it depends more on the particular features of the topic. Once more, when the topic keys into a particular covariance in the vehicle (red and green apples are firm, rotten brown apples are soft), the nature of the transformation differs. Brown balls are seen as softer as a result of this metaphor in contrast to red and green balls.

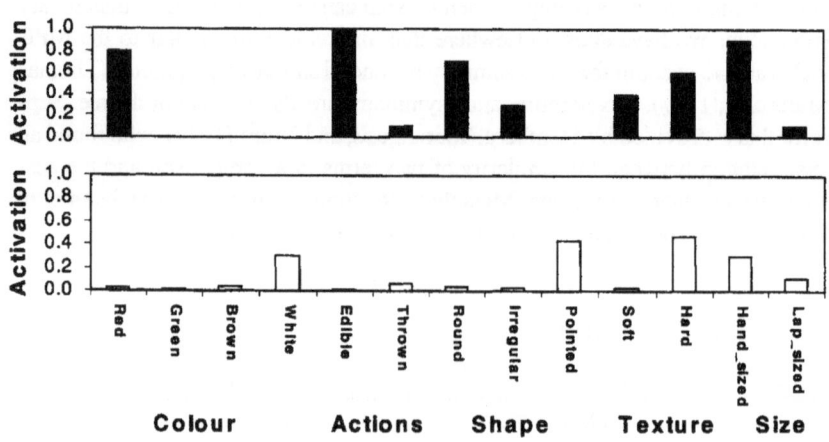

FIGURE 4   When metaphors fail: Interactions between topic and vehicle.

The Red vs Green vs Brown vs White Ball is a Fork

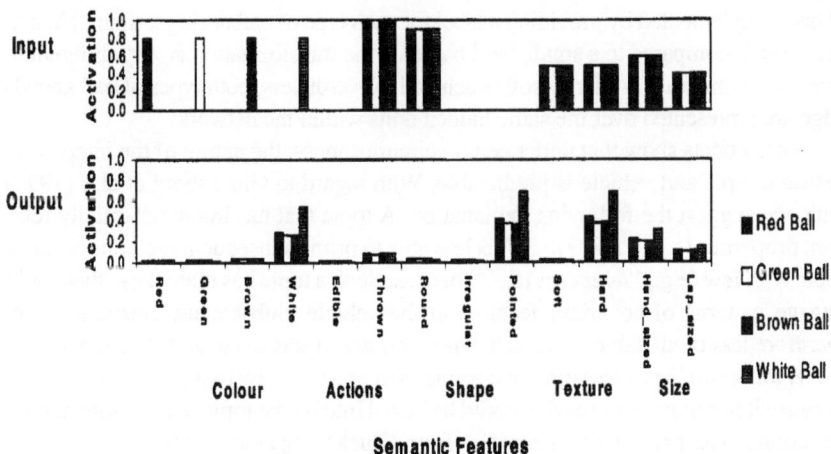

FIGURE 5   The role of the topic in determining the interaction between topic and vehicle.

The Red vs Green vs Brown vs White Ball is an Apple

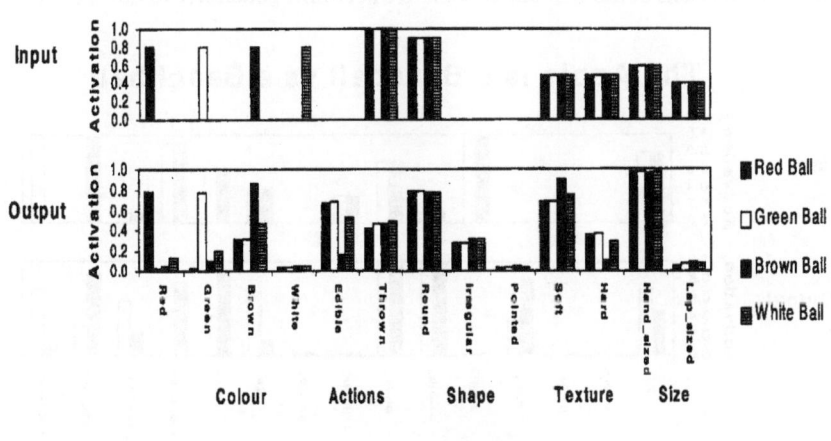

FIGURE 6   The role of the topic in determining the interaction between topic and vehicle.

Figure 7 shows the metaphorical comparison *"the apple is a ball,"* but now supplying contextual information to further specify the type of ball referred to in the vehicle. (This is implemented by providing a label for each type of ball during training.) When the apple is compared to a small, hard baseball, the transformation is very different to when it is compared to a large, soft beach ball. Nevertheless, both types of ball knowledge are represented over the same hidden units within the network.

These effects show that under certain circumstances, the nature of the interaction between topic and vehicle is predictable. With regard to Glucksberg et al.'s (1997) data, we suggest the following explanation. A topic that has many potentially relevant properties (e.g., *"life is a ... "*) is less able to prime subsequent metaphors than a topic with few (e.g., *"temper is a ... "*) because such a topic has many keys that could engage patterns of covariant features in the vehicle. Subsequent interactions are therefore less predictable. A vehicle with a variety of sets of covariant features (e.g., *"... is an ocean"*) is a less effective prime than one with few (e.g., *"... is a crutch"*) because it has more patterns that could be keyed into by the topic. Once more, the interaction is less predictable (examples from Glucksberg et al., 1997).

Further Predictions

Our model makes the following testable predictions. Two phenomena can be predicted on the basis of the way autoassociative networks generalize to novel patterns

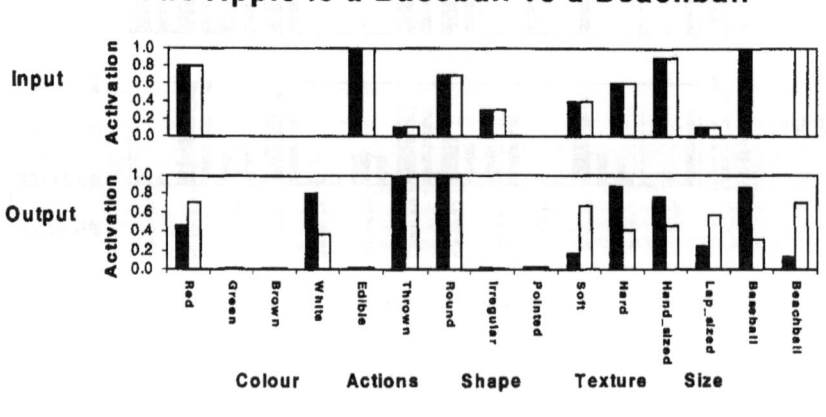

FIGURE 7   The role of the vehicle in determining the interaction between topic and vehicle.

given their training set and the degree of training they have undergone: (a) A lack of variance in the exemplars of the vehicle category will reduce interactivity in metaphor comparisons; that is, it will produce the same transfer of attributes across a range of topics, and (b) in the same way, overtrained or highly familiar vehicles will also generate less interactivity in metaphorical comparisons.

We have proposed an explicit example of how literal and metaphorical comparisons may involve the same type of processing mechanism. However, for a metaphorical comparison, the listener does not accept the full meaning change implied by the comparison, but accepts only features that have been enhanced. This suggests that there is feature change in a metaphorical comparison that is not reported by the participants. For example, in the metaphor *"my rock is a pet,"* we do not conclude that the rock is alive. However, we predict that given a metaphorical comparison, participants will show delayed responses to questions about features of the topic that they would nevertheless not report as aspects of the metaphorical expression (e.g., for *"my rock is a pet,"* the question, Is a rock animate or inanimate?). Evidence for such implicit featural change would support the idea that the reported meaning of a metaphor is the tip of the iceberg of a process of featural enhancement that has much in common with literal language processing.

DISCUSSION

The Relation of Literal to Metaphorical Comparisons

The MPC model uses a categorization device to transfer attributes of the category onto a novel input. Categorization causes a transformation of the input vector to make it more consistent with the category. Metaphor occurs when the novel input is not a member of the category to which it is applied. However, category membership is a graded notion, and categories themselves have internal structure, having more or less typical members (Rosch, 1975).

If we see metaphor as categorization, it only requires a small step to see literal and metaphorical categorization as differing in degree rather than kind. A literal comparison involves categorization of a novel input that is a member of the vehicle category. However, the novel item may be a highly prototypical member of the category. This defines one end of a continuum. The item may be a less typical member, still falling within the category but in some sense being less similar to it. A metaphorical comparison involves an input that has some similarities to the category but falls beyond the normal limits of the category. An anomalous comparison involves an input that falls beyond the normal limits and has few if any similarities to the category.

We propose, then, that literal and metaphorical comparisons are on a continuum of reducing similarity. However, importantly, we propose that literal and metaphorical comparisons are also distinguished by how the semantic distortion caused by the categorization process is then handled. If the change in meaning of the topic caused by the semantic distortion exceeds (context-dependent) expectations, the comparison is taken to be metaphorical, and the communicative intent is taken to refer only to the features of the topic that have been amplified by the transformation. If the threshold is low and we are told that Richard (whom we thought to be a man) is a lion, we are likely to view this claim as literally false and ask for clarification. A higher threshold will cause us to focus only on enhanced features of the topic distortion, viewing the statement as a metaphor. If the threshold expectation of meaning change is very high (e.g., the listener expects the speaker to convey brand new information), then the same statement can be taken as literal and all meaning change accepted as the communicative intent. *"Richard is a lion"* can be false, or it can tell us that a man we know, Richard, is a brave and aggressive man; or it can tell us that a particular lion has been named Richard (a name usually reserved for humans). The actual meaning is not derivable from the comparison alone, but depends on context. Similarly, before context definitively disambiguates the meaning, *"my job is a jail"* could be seen as incongruous (occupations cannot be buildings), or it could tell us that I feel constrained by my job, or it could tell us that my daytime occupation is to act as a physical restraint for some sentient being.

Criticisms of Semantic Feature Explanations of Metaphor

The MPC model is based on simple semantic feature representations of concepts. Such representations have been criticized on a number of grounds as insufficient to explain the processes of metaphor comprehension. In this section, we consider a number of these criticisms. Criticisms 1 through 4 are from Gibbs (1994). Criticism 5 considers the importance of conceptual structure in metaphor comprehension.

Criticism 1.   How can feature-based representations deal with semantically nondeviant representations that are nevertheless metaphorical—that is, those that can have a valid literal interpretation? Our response to this criticism is detailed in the previous section. Simple metaphor comprehension is a two-stage process involving both semantic distortion caused by the juxtaposition and context-dependent interpretation of that distortion.

Criticism 2.   Feature-based representations seem insufficient to deal with the complexities of sophisticated metaphorical expressions. At the moment, this criticism is certainly valid. However, it is also true that we do not know what a more realistic feature-based representation of meaning looks like. The representations in our model are undoubtedly too simple to deal with any more than two-term meta-phors involving attribute mapping. We would expect more realistic and complex feature-based representations to support richer metaphorical distortions in a system following the same principles—that metaphor relies on pattern completion processes invoked through deliberate misclassification.

Criticism 3.   The property transferred from vehicle to topic may not be a property of the vehicle itself (e.g., *"the girl is a lollipop"* may be taken to imply that she is frivolous, but lollipops themselves cannot be described as frivolous). Furthermore, features must not themselves be metaphorical. For example, in the metaphor *"the legislative program was a rocket to the moon,"* we might think this implies that both are fast. However, legislative programs and rockets are not fast in the same way. One response for a feature-based account would be that semantic features are not lexical concepts. That is, in the previous example, a cluster of semantic features defines *fast* for the rocket, and a different cluster, although sharing many of the same features, defines *fast* for a legislative program. Similarly, in *"the girl is a lolli-pop,"* the cluster of features that is enhanced in the representation of girl by the knowledge base for lollipop would share features with the cluster that defines the lexical concept *frivolous.*

The notion that lexical concepts are made up of features is the essence of subsymbolic representation. Features only appear as lexical concepts in our own model for ease of exposition. Thus, *hard* in our model might itself correspond to a set of lower level features, different groups of which would make up different versions of hardness. (See Harris, 1994, for an example of a connectionist model exhibiting subsymbolic, context-dependent meanings of a lexical concept.) Clearly such an account needs to be fleshed out, but we do not believe that this criticism is a terminal one for feature-based representations.

Criticism 4.   Feature overlap accounts do not explain why metaphors have directionality. In the section entitled The Reversibility of Metaphors, we have shown how the model accounts for the directionality of metaphorical comparisons.

Criticism 5.   Feature-based or vector representations cannot deal with relational structure in concepts. Gentner (1988) showed that adults prefer topics and vehicles to be structurally related in metaphors. The model presented here can only address part of the metaphor story, for more complex metaphors will necessarily involve semantic distortions at various levels of conceptual structure. Structured representations are not easily implemented in connectionist systems. However, recent work in the connectionist modeling of analogy formation has shown how feature-based attributes may be dynamically bound to relational structure in a distributed network (Hummel & Holyoak, 1997). Such a network still exploits similarity-based processing and pattern completion in forming and retrieving analogies. Moreover, Henderson and Lane (1998) showed that such dynamically bound representations may be learned in a neural network architecture. We would make two claims. First, we believe that the approach of the MPC model is extendable to structured representations in a connectionist system (similar to that of Hummel & Holyoak, 1997). The principles of such a model would be the same: Metaphor comprehension would rely on pattern completion and subsequent semantic distortion in a system designed for categorization, in this case of structured concepts. Second, we believe it is important to embed such future accounts in neurally plausible learning systems, which minimize the proportion of the theory that relies on arbitrary decisions about the nature of preexisting structured representations (or, indeed, postulates representations with no apparent learnability at all).

An interesting avenue of research will be to explain why children show a shift in preference from attribute mapping to relational mapping during development. Thus far, we have applied the MPC model only to the emergence of the distinction between literal and metaphorical similarity in young children, based on the maturity of their semantic representations (Thomas, Mareschal, & Hinds, 2000). In future work we hope to explore extensions of the model to include relational structure and therefore investigate the developmental shift to more complex metaphors.

CONCLUSION

In this article we have introduced a simple and predominantly illustrative model of how metaphor comprehension may be explained as a form of categorization (Glucksberg & Keysar, 1990, 1993). We have offered the beginnings of an answer to the thorny question of why certain attributes are transferred from the vehicle to the topic in a metaphorical comparison, but not others. The answer was in terms of attributes that the topic possesses that key into covariances of features in the vehicle, and pattern completion processes in a neural network that allow features to be transferred to the topic. This is an essentially interactive account, in line with Black's (1979) favored view of metaphor comprehension. The model is able to offer accounts for recent empirical evidence on the nonreversibility of metaphorical expressions and the nature of the interaction between topic and vehicle (Glucksberg et al., 1997), as well as generating further testable predictions.

Finally, in wider theoretical terms, the model conforms to the notion that metaphor comprehension requires no special processes over and above literal language comprehension by suggesting that metaphorical language and literal language are different points on a continuum of meaning change. Literal and metaphorical statements update comprehension in a different way.

REFERENCES

Black, M. (1955). Metaphor. *Proceedings of the Aristotelian Society, 55,* 273–294.

Black, M. (1962). *Models and metaphors.* Ithaca, NY: Cornell University Press.

Black, M. (1979). More about metaphor. In A. Ortony (Ed.), *Metaphor and thought* (pp. 19–43). Cambridge, England: Cambridge University Press.

Chandler, S. R. (1991). Metaphor comprehension: A connectionist approach to implications for the mental lexicon. *Metaphor and Symbolic Activity, 6,* 227–258.

Fainsilber, L., & Ortony, A. (1987). Metaphorical uses of language in the expression of emotion. *Metaphor and Symbolic Activity, 2,* 239–250.

Gentner, D. (1983). Structure-mapping: A theoretical framework for analogy. *Cognitive Science, 7,* 155–170.

Gentner, D. (1988). Metaphor as structure mapping: The relational shift. *Child Development, 59,* 47–59.

Gentner, D., & Clements, C. (1988). Evidence for relational selectivity in the interpretation of analogy and metaphor. In G. Bower (Ed.), *The psychology of learning and motivation* (Vol. 22, pp. 307–358). Orlando, FL: Academic.

Gibbs, R. W. (1994). *The poetics of mind.* Cambridge, England: Cambridge University Press.

Gibbs, R. W. (1996). Why many concepts are metaphorical. *Cognition, 61,* 309–319.

Gibbs, R. W., & Gerrig, R. (1989). How context makes metaphor comprehension seem "special." *Metaphor and Symbolic Activity, 4,* 154–158.

Glucksberg, S. (1991). Beyond literal meanings: The psychology of allusion. *Psychological Science, 2,* 146–152.

Glucksberg, S., & Keysar, B. (1990). Understanding metaphorical comparisons: Beyond similarity. *Psychological Review, 97,* 3–18.

Glucksberg, S., & Keysar, B. (1993). How metaphors work. In A. Ortony (Ed.), *Metaphor and thought* (2nd ed., pp. 401–424). Cambridge, England: Cambridge University Press.

Glucksberg, S., McGlone, M. S., & Manfredi, D. (1997). Property attribution in metaphor comprehension. *Journal of Memory and Language, 36,* 50–67.

Grice, H. P. (1975). Logic and conversation. In P. Cole & J. Morgan (Eds.), *Syntax and semantics: Vol. 3. Speech acts* (pp. 41–58). New York: Academic.

Harris, C. L. (1994). Back propagation representations for the rule–analogy continuum. In J. A. Barnden & K. J. Holyoak (Eds.), *Advances in connectionist and neural computation theory: Vol. 3. Analogy, metaphor, and reminding* (pp. 282–326). Norwood, NJ: Ablex.

Henderson, J., & Lane, P. (1998). A connectionist architecture for learning to parse. In *Proceedings of COLING-ACL '98* (pp. 531–537). San Francisco: Morgan-Kaufmann Publishers.

Holyoak, K. J., & Thagard, P. (1989). Analogical mapping by constraint satisfaction. *Cognitive Science, 13,* 295–355.

Hummel, J. E., & Holyoak, K. J. (1997). Distributed representations of structure: A theory of analogical access and mapping. *Psychological Review, 104,* 427–466.

Inhoff, A., Lima, S., & Carroll, P. (1984). Contextual effects on metaphor comprehension in reading. *Memory and Cognition, 12,* 558–567.

Lakoff, G. (1987). *Women, fire, and dangerous things: What categories reveal about the mind.* Chicago: University of Chicago Press.

Lakoff, G. (1990). The invariance hypothesis: Is abstract reason based on image-schemas? *Cognitive Linguistics, 1,* 39–74.

Lakoff, G. (1993). The contemporary theory of metaphor. In A. Ortony (Ed.), *Metaphor and thought* (2nd ed., pp. 202–251). Cambridge, England: Cambridge University Press.

Lakoff, G., & Johnson, M. (1980). *Metaphors we live by.* Chicago: University of Chicago Press.

Lakoff, G., & Turner, M. (1989). *More than cool reason: A field guide to poetic metaphor.* Chicago: University of Chicago Press.

Landauer, T. K., & Dumais, S. T. (1997). A solution to Plato's problem: The latent semantic analysis theory of acquisition, induction, and representation of knowledge. *Psychological Review, 104*, 211–240.

Lund, K., & Burgess, C. (1996). Producing high-dimensional semantic spaces from lexical co-occurrence. *Behaviour Research Methods, Instruments and Computers, 2*, 203–208.

McClelland, J. L., & Rumelhart, D. E. (1986). A distributed model of human learning and memory. In J. L. McClelland, D. E. Rumelhart, & The PDP Research Group (Eds.), *Parallel distributed processing: Explorations in the microstructure of cognition: Vol. 2. Psychological and biological models* (pp. 170–215). Cambridge, MA: MIT Press.

McGlone, M. S. (1996). Conceptual metaphors and figurative language interpretation: Food for thought? *Journal of Memory and Language, 35*, 544–565.

McRae, K., Cree, G. S., & McNorgan, C. (1998). Semantic similarity priming without hierarchical category structure. In M. A. Gernsbacher & S. J. Derry (Eds.), *Proceedings of the 20th Annual Meeting of the Cognitive Science Society* (pp. 681–686). Mahwah, NJ: Lawrence Erlbaum Associates, Inc.

Narayanan, S. (1999, July). *Moving right along: A computational model of metaphoric reasoning about events*. Paper presented at the National Conference on Artificial Intelligence, Orlando, FL.

Ortony, A. (1975). Why metaphors are necessary and not just nice. *Educational Theory, 25*, 45–53.

Ortony, A. (1979). Beyond literal similarity. *Psychological Review, 86*, 161–180.

Ortony, A. (1993). The role of similarity in similes and metaphors. In A. Ortony (Ed.), *Metaphor and thought* (2nd ed., pp. 342–356). Cambridge, England: Cambridge University Press.

Ortony, A., Schallert, D., Reynolds, R., & Antos, S. (1978). Interpreting metaphors and idioms: Some effects of context on comprehension. *Journal of Verbal Learning and Verbal Behaviour, 17*, 465–477.

Plaut, D., McClelland, J. L., Seidenberg, M., & Patterson, K. (1996). Understanding normal and impaired reading: Computational principles in quasi-regular domains. *Psychological Review, 103*, 56–115.

Plaut, D., & Shallice, T. (1993). Deep dyslexia: A case study of connectionist neuropsychology. *Cognitive Neuropsychology, 10*, 377–500.

Plunkett, K., Sinha, C., Mueller, M. F., & Strandsby, O. (1992). Symbol grounding or the emergence of symbols? Vocabulary growth in children and a connectionist net. *Connection Science, 4*, 293–312.

Posner, M., & Keele, S. (1968). On the genesis of abstract ideas. *Journal of Experimental Psychology, 77*, 353–363.

Rosch, E. (1975). Cognitive representations of semantic categories. *Journal of Experimental Psychology: General, 104*, 192–223.

Rumelhart, D. E., & McClelland, J. L. (1986). *Parallel distributed processing: Explorations in the microstructure of cognition: Vol. 1. Foundations*. Cambridge, MA: MIT Press.

Searle, J. (1975). Indirect speech acts. In P. Cole & J. Morgan (Eds.), *Syntax and semantics: Vol. 3. Speech acts* (pp. 59–82). New York: Academic.

Small, S. L., Hart, J., Nguyen, T., & Gordon, B. (1996). Distributed representations of semantic knowledge in the brain: Computational experiments using feature based codes. In J. Reggia, E. Ruppin, & R. S. Berndt (Eds.), *Neural modelling of brain and cognitive disorders* (pp. 109–132). London: World Scientific.

Sternberg, R. J., Tourangeau, R., & Nigro, G. (1979). Metaphor, induction, and social policy: The convergence of macroscopic and microscopic views. In A. Ortony (Ed.), *Metaphor and thought* (pp. 277–306). Cambridge, England: Cambridge University Press.

Sun, R. (1995). A microfeature based approach towards metaphor interpretation. In *Proceedings of the 14th International Joint Conference on Artificial Intelligence* (pp. 424–429). San Francisco: Morgan-Kaufmann Publishers.

Thomas, M. S. C., & Mareschal, D. (1997). Connectionism and psychological notions of similarity. In M. G. Shafto & P. Langley (Eds.), *Proceedings of the 19th Annual Conference of the Cognitive Science Society* (pp. 757–762). Mahwah, NJ: Lawrence Erlbaum Associates, Inc.

Thomas, M. S. C., Mareschal, D., & Hinds, A. C. (2000). *A connectionist account of the emergence of the literal-metaphorical-anomalous distinction in young children.* Unpublished manuscript.

Tversky, A., & Gati, I. (1982). Similarity, separability, and the triangle inequality. *Psychological Review, 89,* 123–154.

Veale, T., & Keane, M. T. (1992). Conceptual scaffolding: A spatially founded meaning representation for metaphor comprehension. *Computational Intelligence, 8,* 494–519.

Weber, S. H. (1994). A structured connectionist model of figurative adjective noun combinations. In J. A. Barnden & K. J. Holyoak (Eds.), *Advances in connectionist and neural computation theory: Vol. 3. Analogy, metaphor, and reminding* (pp. 259–281). Norwood, NJ: Ablex.

METAPHOR AND SYMBOL, *16*(1&2), 29–42

Reasoning About Mixed Metaphors Within an Implemented Artificial Intelligence System

Mark G. Lee and John A. Barnden

School of Computer Science
University of Birmingham

The phenomenon of mixed metaphor has traditionally been viewed as secondary to the understanding of straight metaphors. This article suggests that such an assumption is detrimental to long-term research. It is claimed that the same kinds of reasoning and knowledge structures involved in understanding straight metaphors are also required in understanding mixed metaphors and that mixing is a central phenomenon. Therefore, any theory of metaphor must be able to account for mixing. To this end, the article provides an analysis of both parallel and serial mixed metaphors that has been implemented in an artificial intelligence system that is already capable of reasoning about straight metaphors.

Mixed metaphors are often regarded as humorous or as cases of defective speech. Consider the following example, quoted by Fowler (1908) in his guide to writing style:

1. *"This, as you know, was a burning question; and its unseasonable introduction threw a chill on the spirits of all our party."*

The question is metaphorically "hot." However, its introduction makes the party's spirits "cold." Despite this contradiction, the sentence can be understood to mean that the question was somehow controversial and its inappropriate introduction saddened the emotions of the party members. Furthermore, it is plausible that most readers would not even consider the disparity of hot questions causing cold reactions because the two pieces of temperature information could be separately

---

Requests for reprints should be sent to John A. Barnden, School of Computer Science, University of Birmingham, Edgbaston, Birmingham B15 2TT, England. E-mail: J.A.Barnden@cs.bham.ac.uk

mapped to provide connotations relevant in the tenor domain. Owing to these conflicts, such an example makes blending the two metaphors in a single space (as might be advocated by Turner & Fauconnier, 1995) difficult. In this article, we argue that given a mix involving two familiar metaphors for which there are established mappings between the tenor and vehicle domains, the default is that processing is done in two separate "cocoons" (special computational environments).

Under mixed metaphor we include not only examples that might be regarded as obvious cases of conflict, bad style, or humor, but also examples that include graceful combinations of metaphors, such as the following sentence to be examined later: *"One part of John hotly resented the verdict."* This combines a view of John as made up of subagents and a view of agents' emotional states as things that can have temperature. There has been relatively little research done on the topic of mixing due to an assumption that the problem of straight metaphors should be dealt with completely before attempting to tackle the more complex case of mixing. In this article, we argue that this assumption is detrimental to progress because mixed metaphors rely on the same conceptual knowledge as straight metaphors and can, therefore, provide valuable insight into the processes and representations underlying metaphorical reasoning. Moreover, this article makes the following claim: The reasoning processes and data structures involved in understanding mixed metaphors are identical to those used in understanding straight metaphors. Therefore, any current theory of metaphor should (at least in principle) be extensible to deal with mixing.

To this end, we describe some initial work done with ATT-Meta (Barnden, 1997a, 1998; Barnden & Lee, 1999), a computational model of metaphorical comprehension, to handle various types of mixing. We also reprise an earlier claim for the need for extensive within-vehicle reasoning (Barnden, Helmrich, Iverson, & Stein, 1996) and the use of conversion rules to filter the relevant connotations of a particular metaphor.

MIXED METAPHOR DISTINCTIONS

It is possible to distinguish two types of mixed metaphor: parallel mixes and serial mixes. In a *parallel mixed metaphor,* the tenor (A) is seen partly through an *"A as B"* metaphor and partly through another metaphor, *"A as B'."* B and B' are in general different domains, but may overlap. Also, different aspects of A may be involved in the two metaphors. In a *serial mixed metaphor* (commonly called a *chained metaphor*), the tenor (A) is seen as a vehicle (B), which is in turn seen as a different vehicle (C). For example, consider the following two mixed metaphors:

2. *"John's research wounded the theory's shaky foundations."*
3. *"One part of John hotly resented the verdict."*

The utterance in the Example 2 manifests two familiar conceptual metaphors: *"ARGUMENT AS WAR"* (Lakoff & Johnson, 1980), if we construe war in a broad way, and *"THEORIES AS BUILDINGS"* (Grady, 1997; Lakoff & Johnson, 1980). The former is manifested in the verb *wound;* literally, physical living beings wound physical living objects, so both the research and the basic assumptions of the theory are being viewed as physical living beings. However, the theory is also being viewed as a building, and its basic assumptions as physical foundations of it. Following the definition given earlier for parallel mixes, the following domains are involved:

A: Domain of theories, ideas, arguments, and so on.
B: Domain of living beings.
B': Domain of buildings.

Shaky foundations in a building suggest that the building itself might collapse; therefore, if a theory is a building, then its shaky foundations may cause the entire theory to collapse or, literally, be refuted. The sentence is best unraveled by treating the different metaphors (*"A as B,"* *"A as B' "*) separately, because there is conflict between the theory's basic assumptions being viewed as living beings and being viewed as foundations of a building.

The utterance in Example 3 also manifests two familiar conceptual metaphors: *"MIND PARTS AS PERSONS"* (Barnden, 1997b; see also Lakoff, 1996, on metaphors of self and Lakoff, 1993, on *"IDEAS ARE ENTITIES"*) and *"ANGER IS HEAT"* (e.g., Lakoff & Johnson, 1980). In the *"MIND PARTS AS PERSONS"* metaphor, the mind is composed of different person-like parts that may have different beliefs, emotions, and personalities. Mentioning that one part of John resented the verdict suggests that there exists more than one part and that some other part of John did not resent the verdict. Moreover, the part of John referred to resented the verdict *"hotly."* In the *"ANGER AS HEAT"* metaphor, anger is seen as heat. Therefore, the part of John that resented the verdict did so with anger. Hence, if we assume that under *"MIND PARTS AS PERSONS"* the emotions of parts are emotions the whole agent tends to have, John tended to be angry. Following the definitions just given, the following domains are involved:

A: Domain of John's mental and emotional states and processes.
B: Domain of people and natural language communication.
C: Domain of heat.

Example 3 is a serial mixed metaphor. The *"ANGER AS HEAT"* metaphor (B as C) acts on the *"MIND PARTS AS PERSONS"* metaphor (A as B) to directly affect its metaphorical meaning. It is not possible to isolate the two metaphors as in Example 2. It is a mind part that is viewed metaphorically as behaving or feeling hotly, and the mind part is in turn an aspect of a metaphorical view of the topic of John's mind, rather than being directly an aspect of that topic.

Notice also that there is a subtle distinction we wish to capture: Either one part of John is resenting the verdict and one part is not, and the part resenting is doing so *"hotly,"* or both parts of John are resenting the verdict but only one is doing so *"hotly."* Our intuitions suggest that the former interpretation is the default and we only provide a detailed analysis for this interpretation. However, our treatment is sensitive to such distinctions (as is our computational implementation) and is capable of reasoning about such uncertainties.

We gave for Example 2 a parallel mixing interpretation, but we could conceivably give it a serial mixing interpretation instead: According to this, the theory's foundations are viewed as a building as before, and the foundations of the building are then viewed as an animate being, perhaps because of a more generally applicable *"INANIMATE OBJECT AS ANIMATE BEING"* metaphor. However, we view serial mixing as more complex than parallel, so that unless there are pressing reasons to the contrary we prefer to adopt a parallel analysis in case of ambiguity. In any case, given that the parallel analysis is at least a possible one, it is useful to have an account of it.

In contrast, we claim that it is difficult to postulate a parallel reading of Example 3. This is because such a reading would need to view some real component or aspect of John's mind to be viewed as both a subperson and hotly resenting the verdict. However, we claim that the use of *"MIND PARTS AS PERSONS"* carries no implication that the subpersons are mapped to real components or aspects of the mind. Rather, properties of the parts, individually or in conjunction, are mapped to properties of the whole mind. Thus, *"one part of John's mind"* has reference only in vehicle domain B, not the tenor domain.

A COMPUTATIONAL ACCOUNT

The examples discussed in this article are implemented within the ATT-Meta model of metaphor comprehension. We only detail here the concepts relevant to the current work, but further details can be found in works by Barnden (1997a, 1998) and Barnden and Lee (1999).

ATT-Meta is an artificial intelligence (AI) system capable of both simulative reasoning about beliefs and metaphorical reasoning. Reasoning is done by the use of back-chaining rules of inference that allow differing degrees of certainty. Nested reasoning spaces are allowed to facilitate simulation of other agents and metaphorical reasoning. Two types of nested space are maintained: simulation-pretense cocoons and metaphor-pretense cocoons. Simulation-pretense cocoons are used to model the beliefs of other agents. Metaphor-pretense cocoons are a special type of simulation-pretense cocoon in which the agent modeled is a hypothetical agent who is assumed to believe the manifested metaphor is literally true. For the remainder of this article we are concerned only with metaphor-pretense cocoons.

Knowledge of different domains is encoded in sets of facts and rules that apply to a particular domain. Because conceptual metaphors involve a mapping from one domain (the vehicle) to another (the tenor), ATT-Meta uses conversion rules that explicitly map propositions from one domain to another. ATT-Meta has a small set of conversion rules for each metaphorical view it knows about, and it holds knowledge about the vehicle domain of each such view.

Therefore, any conventional metaphor can be defined by constructing a set of rules to represent the vehicle domain plus a suitable conversion rule or a small set of such. Understanding proceeds by creating a metaphor-pretense cocoon (reasoning space) where the manifested metaphor is taken as literally true, then mapping implications to the tenor domain via conversion rules. Figure 1 shows the cocoons involved in parallel and serial mixing schematically.

ATT-Meta is distinctive in that it licenses extensive within-vehicle reasoning in addition to more common, within-tenor reasoning and vehicle-to-tenor mapping. Rather than simply mapping a correspondence from the vehicle to the tenor and then performing inference to fully understand the connotation of an utterance, ATT-Meta favors extensive inference in the metaphor-pretense cocoon prior to mapping in an effort to produce information that can be mapped by conversion rules. This gives any conversion rule the important function of filtering out nonrelevant parts of a particular metaphor. This is essential for metaphor-pretense spaces to be chained in a sensible manner when dealing with difficult examples such as in Example 3.

Parallel Mixed Metaphors

As discussed earlier, Example 2 relies on two familiar conceptual metaphors. Considering the former, *"ARGUMENT AS WAR,"* we assume that ATT-Meta is familiar with the metaphor and so knows the following correspondence:

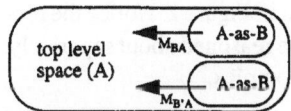

A: Domain of theories (tenor).
B: Domain of living beings (vehicle).
B': Domain of buildings (vehicle').
M_{BA}: Mapping from B to A.
$M_{B'A}$: Mapping from B' to A.

A. Schematic representation of a parallel mix

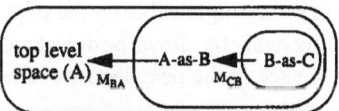

A: Domain of John's mental states (tenor).
B: Domain of people/communication (vehicle).
C: Domain of heat (vehicle).
M_{BA}: Mapping from B to A.
M_{CB}: Mapping from C to B.

B. Schematic representation of a serial mix

FIGURE 1   Arrangement of cocoons (reasoning spaces) for parallel and serial mixed metaphors. The outermost space is the system's top-level reasoning space, in which the tenor domain (A) is reasoned about nonmetaphorically. Other spaces are nested within this. For instance, the cocoon marked as A-as-B is the one for reasoning under the pretense that A really is B.

Metaphorical Correspondence: (Fight-Argue)
Physically damaging an argument/idea/theory/and so on that is being viewed as a battle participant corresponds to establishing faults in the argument/idea/theory/and so on.

This correspondence (and similarly, others later) is couched as a set of conversion rules in ATT-Meta. In addition, suppose ATT-Meta believes the following commonsense rule concerning *"living beings"*:

(Wounding): If X wounds Y then X physically damages Y.

Second, we assume that ATT-Meta is familiar with the metaphor *"THEORIES AS BUILDINGS"* and, as part of this familiarity, knows the following correspondences:

Metaphorical Correspondence: (Instability)
If X is a theory that is being seen as a building then X being unstable corresponds to X being implausible.

Metaphorical Correspondence: (Foundations)
If X is a theory that is being seen as a building then Y being the foundations of X corresponds to Y being the basic assumptions of X.

In addition, ATT-Meta has the following commonsense rule about real buildings:

(Stability): If X is a building and its foundations are shaky, then X is unstable.

Given these mappings and rules, it is possible to infer the connotations that John's research established faults in the theory's basic assumptions and that the theory was implausible by the steps of inference shown in Figure 2. Notice the preceding analysis allows both instances of metaphor to be reasoned about separately. As we see in the next section, serial mixes are more complex.

Serial Mixed Metaphors

As discussed earlier, Example 3 relies on two familiar conceptual metaphors. Considering the former, *"MIND PARTS AS PERSONS,"* we assume that ATT-Meta is familiar with the metaphor and knows the following correspondence:

Metaphorical Correspondence: (State-Tendency)
If person P is viewed as having a part X that is a person, then if X has mental state S then P has a tendency to have state S.

System's top-level reasoning space

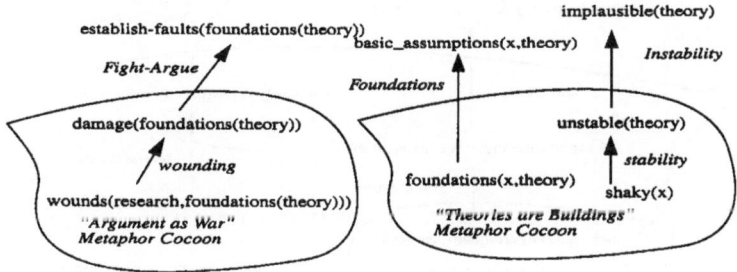

FIGURE 2   Dealing with the parallel mixed metaphor *"John's research wounded the theory's shaky foundations."* Labels next to arrows are rule names used in the text. Notice there is reasoning within the two metaphorical cocoons as well as mapping actions across cocoon boundaries. That reasoning is termed *within-vehicle reasoning* in the text. It can be much more complex and extensive than that shown.

Regarding the second metaphor, *"ANGER AS HEAT,"* it is essential to have the following correspondence:

Metaphorical Correspondence: (HeatisAnger)
Heat proportionally corresponds to emotional anger states.

However, unlike Example 2, it is not possible to deal with each metaphorical manifestation separately. Instead, one cocoon must be nested within the other. Given the rules shown, it is possible to infer the connotation that John had a tendency to angrily resent the verdict by a chain of inference partially shown in the left half of Figure 3.

Given this connotation, it can be argued that Example 3 indirectly implies that another tendency of John is not to angrily resent the verdict. This could be done by a scalar implicature (Hirschberg, 1985) outside the metaphor-pretense cocoon just as if the literal sentence *John had a tendency to angrily resent the verdict* had been uttered instead of the metaphorical one. The reasoning here would not be part of the metaphorical analysis of the sentence. However, another more metaphorical route is as follows: Some general pragmatic implicature is required specifying that when "one" person is mentioned in discourse, then it is reasonable to assume that there is at least one other person present, differing in a salient way from the one mentioned. For the purposes of this article we simplify by using the following defeasible rule:

SeveralPeople:
When one person in a group is explicitly mentioned then there is another person in the group, lacking the mental properties of the first person.

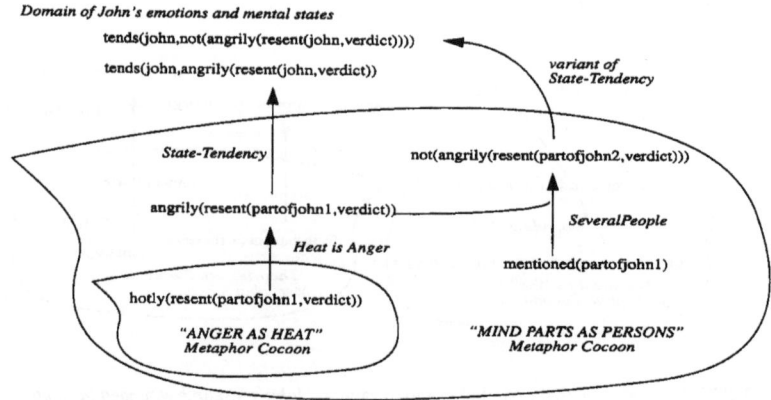

FIGURE 3   Dealing with the serial mixed metaphor *"One part of John hotly resented the verdict."*

Then ATT-Meta can infer within the outer cocoon that there is another subperson of John that does not angrily resent the verdict. From this, a negative variant of State-Tendency can create the inference that John also has tendencies not to angrily resent the verdict. This is sketched on the right-hand side of Figure 3.

The amount of reasoning within cocoons in the examples in this article is quite small and comparable to the extent of within-vehicle reasoning performed by, say, the MIDAS system (Martin, 1990). However, that was partly because of choice of example and partly because of deliberate simplification of the examples for purpose of study. In general, our approach countenances much more elaborate reasoning within cocoons, and this is reflected in the complexity of reasoning involved in other examples we have run ATT-Meta on (see, e.g., Barnden & Lee, 1999).

TOWARD PSYCHOLOGICAL PREDICTIONS

Generating psychological predictions from our model, even in nonmixed cases of metaphor, has not been a major focus of our work to date. However, because in the future some version of ATT-Meta could be put forward as a psychological model, we have in fact been concerned that ATT-Meta should, if possible, be broadly consistent with experimental results in psychology. In particular, we are sensitive to the debate in the psychological literature on metaphor about the relative amounts of time taken by people to understand metaphorical and literal utterances. Brisard, Frisson, and Sandra (2001/this issue) provide one example of work within this debate.

Our approach requires some sort of vehicle-domain meaning (roughly, literal meaning) to be constructed as a base for inference inside the pretense cocoon. It is therefore, in some sense, a "literal first" approach, and some experimental findings have been put forward as conflicting with such approaches (see the literature review in Brisard et al., 2001/this issue). However, note two very important things. First, our approach is not of the type that says that metaphorical connotations are only sought once a literal meaning is discarded. As far as our approach is concerned, a metaphorical utterance could well have one or more literal meanings that make sense in context. Second, measures of whole-utterance reading times or understanding times may well be including a stretch of time for the understander to fully link the utterance to the surrounding discourse and to elaborate the basic compositional meaning of the utterance to get a full communicated proposition. By contrast, the sort of basic literal meaning that goes into the pretense cocoon in our approach does not need to be fully linked or elaborated in the way it would if it were taken to be the point of the utterance. (It may only need certain basic types of linkage, involving, for example, the choice of alternative literal senses for words based on sense choices already made in surrounding discourse.) Rather, it is precisely the within-cocoon reasoning steps and conversion rule applications that serve to link the literal meaning to the meaning of surrounding discourse. Thus, the within-cocoon reasoning and conversion rule applications *replace* discourse linking work that would normally have been done for the literal meaning had it been taken as the point of the utterance. After all, the vehicle-domain inferences that are needed within the cocoon, or inferences like them, could well be needed had the utterance been taken literally in a different context. It may be, therefore, that if our model has an overhead it will lie mainly in the conversion rule applications. However, given that these applications in general only account for a minority of the overall inference steps, the overhead may be minor.

In sum, it is simplistic to assume that a model that espouses the generation of some sort of literal meaning as a basis for the generation of metaphorical meaning, as our model does, has any implication that the processing time needed for the utterance is equal to the time needed to process the utterance *had it been* taken literally plus extra time for doing such operations as metaphorical mapping (e.g., conversion rule application in our terms). It is just such simplistic assumptions that seem to lurk in much writing surrounding psychological experiments on metaphor. Basically, the problem is a simplistic view of what literal meaning is and how it is produced, forgetting in particular the needed discourse linking effort. Honeck, Welge, and Temple (1998) also noted that such effort is usually not discussed.

Having said all this, it is clear that the more it can be shown that metaphorical understanding does often take longer than literal understanding, the less pressure there is on us to put forward these arguments. Here we are encouraged by the results of Brisard et al. (2001/this issue) and others, who do find a slowdown during metaphorical processing. Also, we should note that the psychological results on processing time tend to focus on *"A is B"* style metaphorical utterances. Not only do such utterances form a minority of metaphorical utterances in mundane discourse (as opposed to discussions of metaphor), but also there is reason to think that different forms of metaphorical utterance lead to different timing comparison results (see, e.g., Onishi & Murphy, 1993).

Because the processing in our model is goal directed (see Barnden, 1998; Barnden & Lee, 1999), where the goals are supposed to arise from the processing of context, it is to be expected that the more relevant context there is, the more quickly and easily a given metaphorical utterance embedded within it will be processed. This is broadly consistent with experimental results.

It is not clear that our model currently leads to useful predictions about the particular case of mixed metaphors, other than that the more metaphors that are involved in an utterance, the greater will be the metaphorical slowdown, such as it is. However, any model that did not definitely claim equal time for metaphorical and literal processing would probably predict this.

Finally, we take issue with authors who take equal-time results for figurative and literal understanding to imply that no special type of processing is going on the figurative case. The most that can be inferred from an equal-time result is that if there is special processing, it takes no longer than nonspecial processing does. In any case, what counts as a special type of processing? It is a highly relevant, purpose-sensitive question. For example, is the reasoning inside an ATT-Meta cocoon special? Are conversion rule applications special? The answer to both of these questions is positive, in the sense that a cocoon is involved, and negative to both, in that each individual step is just an inference step of exactly the same computational sort as would be used for literal understanding.

FURTHER DISCUSSION

It is clear that parallel mixes present fewer difficulties to any preexisting theory of metaphor than serial mixes. This is due to the frequent lack of interaction between the two metaphors involved. However, this is not to say that the metaphors in parallel mixing operate in total isolation. Certain parallel mixes are more common than others. In particular, metaphors that refer to abstract entities as physical objects are often mixed with spatial metaphors. For example:

4. *"John pushed the ideas to the back of his mind."*

Example 4 uses two familiar conceptual metaphors: *"IDEAS AS PHYSICAL OBJECTS"* and *"MIND AS ENCLOSED SPACE."* However, it is not clear whether such examples are instances of live mixing. There are two reasons for doubt. First, such examples can often be termed *dead mixes,* mixes that have been so conventionalized that there is no need for any extra reasoning to combine the two familiar metaphors. This, however, is not to suggest that the individual metaphors are dead, only that the mix is so familiar that any metaphorical reasoning is performed in just one meta-phor-pretense cocoon that represents the conventionalized mix of the metaphors.

Second, it is not clear whether the level of representation of conceptual meta-phors is universal. It is conceivable that two different native speakers may repre-sent the same metaphor with different levels of granularity, and, in some cases, a manifestation might be mixed to one speaker and straight to another. Therefore, to avoid such issues, we have adopted a position of methodological solipsism (Fodor, 1980) with respect to the particular set of metaphorical concepts assumed and fo-cused on the actual processes and types of data structures involved in reasoning. Grady (1997) argued that certain metaphors heretofore considered as unitary (in-cluding *"THEORIES AS BUILDINGS,"* in fact) should be regarded as mixes of finer grain metaphors. We agree with this, but there is still the question of which metaphors should be so viewed and how live or dead any mixing is in a given case.

In our brief references to parallel mixing in earlier work (e.g., Barnden, 1997a), we suggested that standard mixes can be handled by having a single metaphori-cal-pretense cocoon, instead of the two assumed in this article. That is, we have pre-viously taken the one-cocoon approach as the default. In this approach, information in the two vehicle domains can interact. This could be seen as a form of blending (Turner & Fauconnier, 1995) with the pretense cocoon acting as the blend space. Sometimes such interaction is benign and easy to perform, and sometimes it is fraught with conflict (as in Examples 1 and 2). It is a matter of further research to rec-oncile the one-cocoon and two-cocoon approaches. One factor that is involved may be the extent of the cognitive resources available: Because the one-cocoon approach may have to deal with conflicts between the two metaphors, it should perhaps only be attempted (in cases of live mixing) when there are cognitive resources to spare.

In serial mixes, the metaphors strongly interact. If the analysis provided earlier is correct, and serial metaphors work by the chaining of one vehicle domain to the other vehicle domain to the tenor, then conversion rules provide an explicit con-straint on what metaphors can be sensibly mixed because a sensible mapping is re-quired from the former vehicle to the latter.

In this view, conversion rules act as filters between domains, first, to constrain the types of serial mixed metaphor possible, and second, to constrain the types of information transferred as only metaphorical manifestations that make sense in the other metaphor-pretense cocoon can be mapped.

In our previous work, it has been assumed that generality in conversion rules and mapping is a good thing. However, given this filtering role, specificity is an advan-tage because it provides strong constraints on mixing. Clearly, within-vehicle rea-soning is important here. If more specific conversion rules are favored, then more of the reasoning workload must be performed prior to mapping to the tenor domain.

In this article, we have dealt exclusively with the mixing of metaphors. However, the mixing of different tropes is also common. For example, Warren (1992) classi-fied five possible combinations of metonymy and metaphor: metaphor within metonyms, metonyms within metaphors, metaphors within metonyms, metaphor in metaphor, and metonyms in metonyms. The only other relevant computational work we are aware of is Fass's (1997) meta* system, which is capable of understanding metonymy and metaphor mixes. (Fass, 1997, also addressed serially mixed metaphor.) In collecting data we have ourselves noted a particular type of metonymy that often occurs in combination with metaphors of mind. An example is *"China was at the surface of John's mind."* Because it is presumably some idea of China, not China itself, that is in the physical space suggested by the "surface of" wording, we have here a combination of a *"THING FOR IDEA OF IT"* metonymy with a *"MIND AS PHYSICAL SPACE"* metaphor. Another interesting example of potential metonymy and metaphor mixing is *"Sally tore Mike's talk to shreds,"* which could variously be interpreted as involving just a metonymy going from the talk to the paper on which the talk was written, so that the tearing is literal, or as involving no metonymy but instead a metaphor of a talk event as a piece of physical fabric, or finally as involving a metonymic link from the talk to the ideas in the talk combined with a metaphor of a body of ideas as a piece of physical fabric.

Also, D. Fass (personal communication, October, 1999) suggested an alternative analysis of Example 3, *"One part of John hotly resented the verdict,"* involving metonymy.[1] Under this analysis, there are two separate "part of" operations in the example: (a) a part of John that is John's emotional and mental states and (b) a part of John's emotional and mental states. Because the explicit mention of "part of" seems to refer to the second sense, the first must be expressed metonymically. Although metonymy is not currently implemented within ATT-Meta, there is no reason why it could not. One future research goal is an analysis of the interaction of metaphor with other tropes such as metonymy. Which particular interpretation is preferred depends on both the context of the metaphor and the particular conceptual knowledge of the hearer.

CONCLUSIONS

In this article, we described some initial work on mixed metaphors. We argued that both parallel and serial mixes can be processed using basic AI reasoning techniques that have already been applied to cases of unmixed metaphor. The serial case requires something extra: the nesting of metaphorical-pretense contexts (cocoons) within each other. However, as the cocoons are similar to the simulative reasoning cocoons also used in ATT-Meta to reason nonmetaphorically about agents' beliefs, and those cocoons also need to be mutually nested, the mutual nesting of metaphorical cocoons is not a conceptually major addition.

---

[1]Despite his analysis being technically possible and consistent with our approach, we find our analysis more plausible owing to its greater simplicity.

We have also suggested that within-vehicle reasoning plays an important role in unmixed metaphor, and this role extends naturally to mixed cases. Indeed, because the point of within-vehicle reasoning is to connect the vehicle-domain content of a metaphorical utterance to vehicle-domain concepts that the known mappings can directly handle (to avoid as far as possible the expensive process of discovering new mappings), within-vehicle reasoning plays a particularly important role in mixing because of the higher number of domains being juggled. Questions for further research include that of criteria for choosing to pursue a serial interpretation versus a parallel one, and that of criteria for deciding during processing in the parallel case whether to use one metaphorical-pretense cocoon or two.

ACKNOWLEDGMENTS

This research is being supported in part by Grant GR/M64208 from the Engineering and Physical Sciences Research Council, England, and has previously been supported by Grant IRI–9101354 from the National Science Foundation.

REFERENCES

Barnden, J. A. (1997a). An AI system for metaphorical reasoning about mental states in discourse. In J.-P. Koenig (Ed.), *Conceptual structure, discourse and language* (Vol. 2, pp. 167–188). Stanford, CA: Center for the Study of Language and Information.

Barnden, J. A. (1997b). Consciousness and common-sense metaphors of the mind. In S. O'Nuallain, P. McKevitt, & E. Mac Aogain (Eds.), *Two sciences of the mind: Readings in cognitive science and consciousness* (pp. 311–340). Amsterdam: Benjamins.

Barnden, J. A. (1998). Combining uncertain belief reasoning and uncertain metaphor-based reasoning. In M. A. Gernsbacher & S. J. Derry (Eds.), *Proceedings of the 20th Annual Meeting of the Cognitive Science Society* (pp. 114–119). Mahwah, NJ: Lawrence Erlbaum Associates, Inc.

Barnden, J. A., Helmrich, S., Iverson, E., & Stein, G. C. (1996). Artificial intelligence and metaphors of mind: Within-vehicle reasoning and its benefits. *Metaphor and Symbolic Activity, 11,* 101–123.

Barnden, J. A., & Lee, M. G. (1999). An implemented context system that combines belief reasoning, metaphor-based reasoning and uncertainty handling. In P. Bouquet, P. Brezillon, & L. Serafini (Eds.), *Modelling and using context* (Lecture Notes in Artificial Intelligence, No. 1688, pp. 28–41). Berlin, Germany: Springer-Verlag.

Brisard, F., Frisson, S., & Sandra, D. (2001/this issue). Processing unfamiliar metaphors in a self-paced reading task. *Metaphor and Symbol, 16,* 87–108.

Fass, D. (1997). *Processing metonymy and metaphor.* Greenwich, CT: Ablex.

Fodor, J. A. (1980). Methodological solipsism considered as a research strategy in cognitive psychology. *Behavioural and Brain Sciences, 3,* 63–109.

Fowler, H. W. (1908). *The king's English* (2nd ed.). Oxford, England: Clarendon.

Grady, J. E. (1997). Theories are buildings revisited. *Cognitive Linguistics, 8,* 267–290.

Hirschberg, J. (1985). *A theory of scalar implicature.* Unpublished doctoral dissertation, University of Pennsylvania, Philadelphia.

Honeck, R. P., Welge, J., & Temple, J. G. (1998). The symmetry control in tests of the standard pragmatic model: The case of proverb comprehension. *Metaphor and Symbol, 13*, 257–273.

Lakoff, G. (1993). The contemporary theory of metaphor. In A. Ortony (Ed.), *Metaphor and thought* (2nd ed., pp. 202–251). New York: Cambridge University Press.

Lakoff, G. (1996). Sorry, I'm not myself today: The metaphor system for conceptualizing the self. In G. Fauconnier & E. Sweetser (Eds.), *Spaces, worlds, and grammar* (pp. 91–123). Chicago: University of Chicago Press.

Lakoff, G., & Johnson, M. (1980). *Metaphors we live by.* Chicago: University of Chicago Press.

Martin, J. H. (1990). *A computational model of metaphor interpretation.* San Diego, CA: Academic.

Onishi, K. H., & Murphy, G. L. (1993). Metaphoric reference: When metaphors are not understood as easily as literal expressions. *Memory and Cognition, 21*, 763–772.

Turner, M., & Fauconnier, G. (1995). Conceptual integration and formal expression. *Metaphor and Symbolic Activity, 10*, 183–204.

Warren, B. (1992). *Sense developments: A contrastive study of the development of slang senses and novel standard senses in English.* Stockholm: Almqvist & Wiksell.

METAPHOR AND SYMBOL, *16*(1&2), 43–57
Copyright © 2001, Lawrence Erlbaum Associates, Inc.

Metaphors, Logic, and Type Theory

Josef van Genabith

School of Computer Applications
Dublin City University

Metaphorical use of language is often thought to be at odds with compositional, truth-conditional approaches to semantics: After all, most metaphors are literally false. In this article we sketch an approach to metaphors based on standard type theory. Our approach is classical: We do not invent a new logic. The approach models sense extension in a simple and elegant way: The properties (supertypes) shared between tenor and vehicle include the extensions of at least both. The original predicates remain unchanged. Our approach captures an asymmetry between metaphor and simile. The literal interpretation of a metaphor comes out as (mostly) false, whereas its nonliteral interpretation is that of a corresponding reduced simile. A compositional syntax–semantics interface is provided and a deductive account of metaphor resolution is outlined. The approach readily translates into a simple computational implementation in Prolog. We discuss how our approach addresses issues of generalization, feature selection, asymmetry, tension, trivialization, prototypicality, truth conditions, comprehension, and generativeness.

Nonliteral use of language such as metaphor is usually thought to sit uneasily with formal, truth-conditional semantics in the Montagovian tradition (Montague, 1973). Most metaphors are simply literally false.[1] Consider, for example, the following established metaphor, its formalization in first-order predicate logic (FOPL;

Requests for reprints should be sent to Josef van Genabith, School of Computer Applications, Dublin City University, Dublin 9, Ireland. E-mail: josef@compapp.dcu.ie

[1]This is the reason why simple meaning postulates (axioms) are of limited use in treatments of metaphor. The problem is the following: Consider the metaphorical sentence in Example 1. Assume that it translates as *fox(j)*. Assume further that, for the sake of the argument, we have an axiom stating that all foxes are clever. From these we can deduce *fox(j)*, $\forall x(fox(x) \rightarrow clever(x)) \vdash clever(j)$ as a possible interpretation of Example 1. This inference is fine even if an additional *human(j)* axiom is in force. However, things start turning sour as soon as we have another axiom in place that states that the sets of humans and foxes are disjoint: $\forall x \neg(human(x) \land fox(x))$. Given this and our previous assumptions, inconsistency strikes: We can prove $human(j) \land \neg(human(j))$, or indeed any conclusion we wish. The approach developed in this article avoids such pitfalls.

in FOPL, quantification is restricted to range over individuals), and associated truth conditions:

1. "John is a fox." $| fox(j) | [fox(j)] = 1$ iff $[j] \in [fox]$

The formula $fox(j)$ can be glossed as follows: The one-place predicate fox (the FOPL translation of *fox*) is predicated of the logical constant j (the FOPL translation of *John*). Equivalently, the formula states that j has the property fox. Formulas in FOPL are interpreted in models. A model is a set theoretic construct consisting of a universe of interpretation (a set of objects; also referred to as the domain) and an interpretation function that specifies which constants are interpreted as which objects in the universe and which predicates are interpreted as which subsets (of individuals or n-tuples, depending on the number n of arguments particular predicates take) in the universe. The interpretation of a constant or predicate symbol is also variously referred to as the denotation or extension of the constant or the predicate symbol. A model fixes the interpretation of basic constituent expressions (the vocabulary, if you like). Complex expressions (i.e., formulas) are interpreted in terms of a recursively specified function (often represented as [.]) that follows the syntactic formation rules of FOPL. The base cases of this function are provided by the interpretation of constants and predicate symbols given by the model.

On this account the interpretation of Example 1 is true if and only if the denotation $[j]$ of the logical constant j (the translation of John) is an element of the denotation $[fox]$ of the one-place predicate fox (the translation of fox). Put differently, Example 1 is true if and only if $\{[j]\} \cap [fox] \neq 0$.

This, however, is not the case that obtains in the literal reading of Example 1 involving, as it does, a predication of a property to an individual not in the extension of the property predicated (to be fully explicit, here we are, of course, assuming that John is human). Several responses are possible. For all their differences, most approaches to metaphor assume that metaphor invites the determination of a similarity or likeness between tenor and vehicle. One line of thought maintains that metaphor is a comparison statement (Aristotle, 1952) that can be analyzed as a reduced or elliptical simile (Fogelin, 1988). In these accounts, Example 1 corresponds to Example 2 paraphrased in Example 3, or, following Black's (1962) "system of associated commonplaces," to Example 4, paraphrased in Example 5:

2. "John is like a fox."
3. "John has some of the properties of foxes."
4. "John is like a typical fox."
5. "John has some of the typical properties of foxes."

Paraphrases 3 and 5 are readily translatable into standard type theory (Church, 1940) and a compositional syntax–semantics interface can be set up. This will allow us to parse natural language strings automatically into literal and metaphorical meaning representations, and this is one of the themes developed in this article. Standard type theory is a higher order logic (HOL) based on the typed λ-calculus. HOL (rather than FOPL) is required because Paraphrases 3 and 5 quantify over properties... some of the properties ... (i.e., sets) rather than just individuals. Versions of HOL have been the standard choice of representation formalism in much formal semantics in the Montagovian tradition.

Interpretation of metaphor as corresponding reduced simile has been objected to on a number of grounds. We discuss how our approach addresses issues of generalization, feature selection, asymmetry, tension, trivialization, prototypicality, truth conditions, comprehension, and generativeness.

TYPE THEORY TT

The type theory TT we employ is little more than a sugared version of the typed λ-calculus (see, e.g., Church, 1940; Gamut, 1991). The basic idea in type theory is that, based on a set of primitive types (in the simplest version a type e of entities—or individuals—and a type t of truth values), logical connectives, predicates, arguments, and quantifiers are represented in terms of functions over those basic types. For example, n place relations can easily be coded as $n + 1$ place functions. The typing regime is designed to avoid paradoxes and inconsistencies that could otherwise arise due to the considerable expressive power of HOL. In what follows, we briefly sketch simple extensional type theory, which provides our representation formalism. The set of types T is defined as $e, t \in T$ and if $a, b \in T$ then $\langle a, b \rangle \in T$ (this is the type of functions from type a objects to type b objects). The basic vocabulary of TT has sets of variables Var_τ and constants Con_τ, for each $\tau \in T$. The syntax closes TT under application, abstraction, the logical connectives, and quantification. Interpretation is relative to models $\mathcal{M} = \langle \mathcal{D}, \mathcal{J} \rangle$ where $\mathcal{D}$ is a domain of individuals and $\mathcal{J}$ an interpretation function interpreting constant symbols. Types are interpreted as function spaces (domains). Interpretation domains $\mathcal{D}_\tau$ for types τ are defined as $\mathcal{D}_e := \mathcal{D}$, $\mathcal{D}_t := \{0, 1\}$ and $\mathcal{D}_{\langle a, b \rangle} := \mathcal{D}_b^{\mathcal{D}_a}$. Given a model $\mathcal{M} = \langle \mathcal{D}, \mathcal{J} \rangle$ with $\mathcal{J}: Con_\tau \to \mathcal{D}_\tau$ g: $Var_\tau \to \mathcal{D}_\tau$ (for each type τ) the interpretation function [.] is defined as follows:[2]

1. $[c_a]^{\mathcal{M}, g} = \mathcal{J}(c_a)$; $[x_a]^{\mathcal{M}, g} = g(x_a)$
2. $[\varphi_{\langle a, b \rangle} (\psi_a)]^{\mathcal{M}, g} = [\varphi_{\langle a, b \rangle}]^{\mathcal{M}, g} ([\psi_a])^{\mathcal{M}, g})$
3. $[\lambda x_a \varphi_b]^{\mathcal{M}, g}$ is that function h such that for all $u \in \mathcal{D}_a$, $h(u) = [\varphi_b]^{\mathcal{M}, g(x/u)}$
4. $[\neg \varphi_t]^{\mathcal{M}, g}$ iff $[\varphi_t]^{\mathcal{M}, g} = 0$

---

[2]The remaining connectives and quantifiers are defined from these in the usual fashion: $\varphi \vee \psi \equiv \neg(\neg\varphi \wedge \neg\psi)$, $\varphi \to \psi \equiv \neg(\varphi \wedge \neg\psi)$, $\exists x \varphi \equiv \neg \forall x \neg \varphi$

5. $[(\varphi_t \wedge \psi_t)]^{M,g} = 1$ iff $[\varphi_t]^{M,g} = 1$ and $[\psi_t]^{M,g} = 1$

6. $[\forall x_a \varphi t]^{M,g} = 1$ iff for all $u \in \mathcal{D}_a [\varphi_t]^{M,g\,(x/u)} = 1$

Axiomatizations of *TT* are incomplete under interpretation in standard models (admitting the full function spaces). Sound and complete axiomatizations of *TT* are provided for general models (Henkin, 1950). For readability, we often suppress type annotations in the following formulas.

EXPRESSING SIMILES IN *TT*

On the most natural reading of the simile interpretation (Example 2) of Example 1, the object noun phrase is given a generic (*all/most/typical/bare plural*) interpretation:

6. "John has a property which is a property of (all/most/typical) foxes."

For expository purposes and reasons of space, in the following we approximate the generalizability of the object noun phrase argument by simple universal quantification. More sophisticated (and appropriate) treatments are possible (see, e.g., Carlson & Pelletier, 1995), and in a later section we outline an interpretation based on a prototype (i.e., a cultural stereotype) analysis. With this proviso, Example 6 is approximated by the following *TT* expression:

7. $\exists P(P j \wedge \forall x(fox\ x \rightarrow Px))$

This *TT* formula can be glossed as follows: There exists a property P that holds of j and P is a property of all foxes. Example 7 comes out true if there exists a property P (simple or complex) denoting a subset of the domain of entities that includes both the extension of j and the (members of the) extension of the *fox* predicate:

8. $[\exists\ P(P j \wedge \forall x\ (fox\ x \rightarrow Px\ ))] = 1$ iff there exists a P such that $[fox] \cup \{[j]\} \subseteq [P]$

SENSE EXTENSION, SUPERTYPES, GENERALIZATION, AND FEATURE SELECTION

Our analysis captures sense extension in a simple and elegant way. The extension of P is a set that minimally includes both the extension of j and the elements in the extension of *fox*. Notice, however, that the extension of the original *fox* predicate itself remains unchanged. The property P is what extends *fox* and additionally includes at least the extension of j. P is a supertype of *fox* and the minimal type that includes j. In other words, P generalizes *fox* and the minimal type that includes j.

If instead we had opted for a nonclassical approach and extended the denotation of the *fox* property itself to include that of j, we would be faced with the following problem: Assume that all foxes have bushy tails. If the extension of *fox* were to include that of j, we could prove that John has a bushy tail, clearly an undesirable result if, as we are assuming in our metaphor scenario, John is decidedly a member of homo sapiens. Worse, if our axiomatization of background knowledge includes a statement to the effect that John is human as well as a statement that the categories human and fox are disjoint, then extending the *fox* predicate to include j leads to inconsistency. Notice that given the same scenario in our approach such inferences do not go through. Example 7 constrains the shared property P to hold of both the (original) set of foxes and (the disjoint singleton set of) John. Assuming that John is human, the joint property P cannot be instantiated to that of having a bushy tail. If it was, it would falsify the conjunction in Example 7. Similarly, inconsistency of the form just described cannot arise because our approach does not extend the *fox* predicate.

Notice further that our analysis naturally captures a feature selection process often attributed to metaphor, most famously perhaps in Black's (1962) analogy between metaphor interpretation and looking at the stars through an etched piece of smoked glass. Whatever the property variable P is instantiated to, Example 7 minimally requires that it generalizes the *fox* property and the properties of John. That is, the property abstracts away from what is idiosyncratic to the *fox* property and j to find properties that are common to both. This is, of course, related to the point raised earlier and the reason properties that are not shared (e.g., having a bushy tail) are suppressed. Feature selection theories have been refined to include graded salience mechanisms (e.g., Ortony, 1979; Thomas & Mareschal, 1999) that can be addressed by extending our approach to probability logics (e.g., Adams, 1998).

YOU CANNOT SEE WHAT IS NOT THERE ... TRUTH CONDITIONS AND ASYMMETRY

On the other hand, our analysis requires that P can only be instantiated to shared properties that are already there. To use Black's (1962) analogy once again, in this approach the smoked glass (and its clear lines) will not allow you to see things that are not there in the first place. You might not have been aware of them, but they have been there all along. It is important to notice that first and foremost the analysis developed in this article provides a truth conditional account of metaphorical meaning analyzed as reduced simile. It does not provide an account of an agent processing a metaphor. Logic can, of course, be used to extend it to one: intuitionistic, constructive, modal, and dynamic logics provide natural settings for modeling information growth and update (e.g., Jaspars, 1994; Vogel, 2001/this issue). For our purposes here we follow a more confined program. In a later section we provide a deductive account of metaphor resolution (i.e., instantiation of P relative to an existing axiomatization of background knowledge).

On closer inspection, although not obvious, it has often been observed that metaphors are asymmetric (Ortony, 1979): "lawyers are sharks" is not the same as "sharks are lawyers." By contrast, our approach is symmetric. Again, this is because the account developed here provides truth conditions and not a model of the dynamics of an agent's knowledge states under metaphor comprehension.

TENSION, TRIVIALIZATION, MINIMAL EXTENSION, AND PROTOTYPICALITY

Tension is a characteristic quality attributed to metaphor (e.g., Davidson, 1984). Tension derives from the fact that (a) most metaphors are literally false, (b) literal meaning is still active in nonliteral interpretation, and (c) metaphors have an open-ended quality (i.e., precisely which meaning is intended is uncertain). These aspects feature in the analysis offered here: The literal meaning of Example 1 is $fox(j)$, literal meaning components (fox, j) feature prominently in the representation of the nonliteral meaning of Example 1 in Example 7, and the shared property P is existentially quantified; that is, we know there should be some property that is shared by tenor and vehicle, but we do not know exactly which one.

Open-endedness of interpretation, one of the characteristic qualities of metaphor, does not extend to trivial likeness. In fact, trivial likeness has been fielded against analyzing metaphor as elliptical simile (Davidson, 1984): "everything is like everything and in endless ways" (p. 254). Although I disagree with Davidson, whose objection relies on (a) the implication that if similarity was trivial then all similarity statements would be trivial, and (b) the false premise that similarity is trivial (the second premise is contradicted by the fact that in most communicative situations where agents use similarity statements the intended and communicated similarity is entirely nontrivial; in other words, similarity is a useful concept), triviality does indeed strike at the formal level. Notice that the domain of interpretation (the set of entities) is a set that trivially includes the extension of j and the extension of the fox predicate. From this it follows that a universal property such as $\lambda x.\ x = x$ (the property of being identical to oneself) trivially satisfies Example 7. Although it is arguable that trivialization is the limit case of nonliteral use of language, trivialization of this kind can be ruled out by strengthening the translation to require that P not be instantiated to a universal property, for example:

9. $\exists P(Pj \wedge \forall x(fox\ x \rightarrow Px) \wedge \neg\ \forall yPy)$.

Although this move rules out the most trivial (i.e., the universal) properties and ensures that Example 9 is contingent, it still admits possibly infinitely many other shared, potentially trivial properties such as, for example, the property of not being identical to my fridge[3] (or indeed any entity described in a background knowledge axiomatization other than John or any of the foxes). Notice, however, that such inferences crucially depend on a $\mathcal{K}^i \neq \mathcal{K}^j$ for $i \neq j$ (where $\mathcal{K}$ is a metavariable over constant symbols of type e) axiom schema. The schema is optional and requires that distinct constant symbols are interpreted as distinct entities. If we want to rule out a possible interpretation of Example 1 as "John is similar to foxes in that they are all not the same as my fridge" (which in some bizarre context might in fact be the desired interpretation), we need to switch off (i.e., ignore) the constant axiom schema (if present). Formally this corresponds to structure mapping approaches to metaphor (Falkenheiner, Forbus, & Gentner, 1989; Veale & Keane, 1992) not, or only selectively, or only implicitly encoding inequality statements of the sort at stake. Everything else being equal, the type-theory-based approach developed here and the structure-mapping-based approaches are generative. They will produce as many interpretations as are admitted by their background knowledge axiomatizations or (in the case of the mapping approaches) knowledge graphs. Generative capacity can be curtailed or extended by axioms or restrictions on proof depth (both options are in fact availed of by mapping approaches in the form of selective knowledge graph coding and limits on recursive computations and graph matches). In addition, in the type theory approach we can curtail generative capacity by strengthening the translation, as in Example 9. As a further example, consider how a translation can enforce a notion of minimal extension:

10. $\exists P(Pj \land \forall x(fox\ x \rightarrow Px) \land \forall Q((Qj \land \forall x(fox\ x \rightarrow Qx)) \rightarrow (Pj \rightarrow Qj)))$.

This translation of Example 1 requires that the joint property P shared between tenor and vehicle is minimal in the sense that P implies all other shared properties Q.

Before moving on to prototypicality, notice that in contrast to some other feature-based approaches (e.g., Thomas & Mareschal, 1999), our type theory approach does not distinguish between simple and complex properties. (In type theory, complex properties model relations and relational structure; for example, Example 14.) Indeed, from the type theory perspective such a distinction is somewhat artificial. In our approach the properties generated are those that can be proved from whatever is axiomatized. These include simple and complex ones. It is here (in the complex properties) that recursive submetaphors can get involved in an interpretation.

In our translations so far we have assumed that the vehicle contributes a generic or a typical property (and in fact we have glossed over the difference between the

---

[3]This example was provided by one of the anonymous reviewers.

generic and the typical and, for expository purposes approximated both in terms of universal quantification). It has been observed (e.g., Black, 1962) that often what is at stake in metaphor interpretation is cultural stereotypes taking the form of stereotypical individuals or prototypes, rather than definitions of classes in terms of necessary and sufficient conditions. In this account, Example 1 is likely to be interpreted as stating that "John is clever" and this interpretation derives from comparing John to a prototype *fox*. In the words of one of the anonymous reviewers: "The metaphor compares John to an archetype of fox, a cultural model that owes as much to Aesop as to Darwin." This intuition can be integrated into the type theoretic approach. An axiomatization of the cultural stereotype *fox* is required. To do this with any degree of confidence requires a psycholinguistic or cognitive theory of cultural stereotypes or prototypes, which is beyond the more confined concerns of this article. Give such an axiomatization in the form of, for example, *prty fox P* statements where not surprisingly *prty* (short for prototype) is of the type of a generalized quantifier (Barwise & Cooper, 1981) ($\langle\langle e,t\rangle,\langle\langle e,t\rangle,t\rangle\rangle$) pairing a property (i.e., a class, here *fox*[4], with its perceived prototypical properties *P*), the metaphorical meaning of Example 1 is captured by:

11. $\exists P(Pj \wedge prty\ fox\ P)$

This translation guarantees that the shared property derives from the axiomatization of the prototypical concept *fox*, which is often what is encoded in the knowledge graphs in structure mapping approaches.

In the next section we show how our analysis generalizes from simple copula constructions to more complex predications.

COMPLEX PREDICATIONS

The formulae in Examples 7, 9, and 10 encode a simple supertype and sense extension analysis of metaphors involving predicative uses of the copula be. As pointed out, any instantiation of the unary predicate *P* that makes Examples 7, 9, and 10 true denotes a superset including both the denotation of *j* and the elements in the denotation of *fox*. It is here that the sense extension dimension of metaphor is located in our approach. The basic idea can easily be generalized to cover more complex predications as exemplified by this well-worn example:

12. "My car drinks gasoline."

---

[4]The class *fox* stands proxy for a prototypical individual. *Prty* simply pairs the class with its perceived cultural stereotypes.

To a first approximation and following the lead of the approach developed earlier, the nonliteral use of this example can be paraphrased as

13. "My car and gasoline stand in a relation that is a property of all drink relations."

The relation in question is probably something like the *consume* relation. Every drink event is also a consume event (but not vice versa). Example 13 is readily formalizable. Here we translate the definite possessive noun phrase my car as the constant c and simplify the mereological noun phrase gasoline as g.[5]

14. $\exists R(Rgc \wedge \forall x \forall y(drink\, yx \rightarrow Ryx))$

R is of type $\langle e, \langle e, t \rangle \rangle$; that is, it is a binary relation between entities. As was the case with the simple predication in Example 7, Example 14 is trivialized by the universal relation $\Re$ (where, e.g., x is related to y if x is identical with itself and y is identical with itself). Following Example 9, this can be ruled out as follows:

15. $\exists R(Rgc \wedge \forall x \forall y(drink\, yx \rightarrow Ryx) \wedge \neg \forall x \forall y Ryx)$.

Following the approach developed in the previous section, the translation can be strengthened to requiring minimal or prototypical instances of two-place relations R relative to *drink*. The *consume* relation provides one of the instantiations of R in Example 14. Notice that Example 14 fixes a potential selection restriction violation between *drink* and its subject noun phrase (*–animate*). Assume that *drink* subcategorizes for a (*+animate*) subject noun phrase. Example 14 forces R to generalize *drink* so that it can apply to my car (*–animate*) and gasoline. Furthermore, by itself Example 14 does not support any inference as to excessive amounts of consumption often attributed to Example 12. Example 12 is similar to the following, which was suggested by one of the anonymous referees as a challenge for the approach:

16. "I wrestled with the idea."

Appendix A provides a Prolog implementation of a compositional syntax–semantics interface. Appendix B extends this to treat Example 16 as analogous to Example 12.

---

[5]Readers unfamiliar with the functional type theory notation may be puzzled by the order of arguments in $R\,g\,c$ in Example 14. The contribution g of the direct object comes first, followed by the contribution c of the subject. In the Prolog implementations in Appendices A and B we switch back to the familiar relational representations: R(c,g).

17. "Myself and the idea stand in a relation that is a
property of all wrestling relations."

RESOLUTION

The reduced simile reading $\exists P(Pj \wedge \forall x(fox\ x \to Px))$ of Example 1 is weak and trivialized by the universal property. Trivialization can be excluded in a number of ways, as exemplified in Examples 9, 10, and 11. Trivial use of simile (and metaphor in the reduced simile account) in actual communicative situations is probably quite rare.[6] What makes simile and metaphor interesting is the task of finding nontrivial (i.e., informative) instances of the property P shared between tenor and vehicle. From the existentially quantified formula offered as a reduced simile reading of Example 1, we cannot deduce much: Existential quantification over P amounts to a (possibly infinite) disjunction over suitable predicates of the type of P whose extension is required to include both tenor and vehicle. However, rather than deriving inferences from the reduced simile reading, we can look for proofs that, given some background theory (premises in a knowledge base), allow us to deduce the reduced simile reading. Such proofs contain candidate instances of shared properties that enable us to existentially quantify over them. Consider the following simple example (we use the universal quantification approximation of genericity):

$$clever\ j,\ \forall x(fox\ x \to clever\ x) \vdash \exists\ P(Pj \wedge \forall x(fox\ x \to Px))$$

To find suitable resolvents $[P = clever]$, we have to inspect proofs. The question is whether there is a systematic (i.e., automatic) way of searching for and inspecting such proofs. A signed tableaux proof of this inference looks as follows:

1 T	*clever j*	
2 T	$\forall x(fox\ x \to clever\ x)$	
3 F	$\exists P[Pj \wedge \forall x(fox\ x \to Px)]$	
4 F	$clever\ j \wedge \forall x(fox\ x \to clever\ x)$	
5 F	$clever\ j\ \mid$	6F $\forall x(fox\ x \to clever\ x)$

The trick here is, of course, in the step from line 3 to line 4 in the tableaux. We know that to close the tableaux we need to find formulas corresponding to lines 1 and 2 but signed *F*. However, ideally, we do not want to rely on human intelligence and insight to guide and inspect proofs. This is where free variable tableaux come to the rescue.

---

[6]This is mostly confined to jokes.

Without going into great detail (Fitting, 1996), the basic idea is to delay instantiation of especially introduced variables as long as possible in the development of a tableaux, ideally until closure of a branch. Tracking such variables provides candidate resolutions. A free variable tableaux version of our proof is given here (the predicate variable introduced in going from Step 3 to 4 is Π):

$$
\begin{array}{lll}
1\,\text{T} & & clever\ j \\
2\,\text{T} & & \forall x(fox\ x \rightarrow clever\ x) \\
3\,\text{F} & & \exists P[Pj \wedge \forall x(fox\ x \rightarrow Px)] \\
4\,\text{F} & & \Pi j \wedge \forall x(fox\ x \rightarrow \Pi x) \\
\hline
5\,\text{F} & \Pi j\ | & 6\text{F}\ \forall x(fox\ x \rightarrow \Pi x)
\end{array}
$$

This tableaux can be closed by matching lines 5 and 1, and lines 4 and 2, thereby instantiating Π to *clever,* which yields a candidate resolution of P.

Notice that there is a striking parallel between our deductive approach and structure mapping ($\mathcal{SM}$) approaches such as those in Falkenheiner et al. (1989) and Veale and Keane (1992), summarized as:

$\mathcal{LOGIC}$:	Premises	$\vdash$	Reduced Simile
$\mathcal{SM}$:	Knowledge Base Graph	$\supset$	Metaphor Graph

where $\supset$ is subgraph isomorphism. What differentiates the two approaches is that structure mapping approaches usually intend to give an account of the dynamics of metaphor comprehension, whereas our approach explicates truth conditions. As pointed out, logic (intuitionistic, modal, or dynamic) can be used to model the dynamics of comprehension, but this is beyond the more narrow confines of this article.

A COMPOSITIONAL SYNTAX–SEMANTICS INTERFACE

In this section we show that the different readings (both literal and metaphorical) associated with Examples 1 and 12 do not come out of thin air but can be computed in a systematic fashion given a syntactic analysis of the strings at stake. A compositional syntax–semantics interface is specified by a pairing of syntactic formation and semantic translation rules and a specification of the translation of lexical elements. The translation function is indicated $^\circ$:

$$
\begin{array}{lll}
S & \rightarrow\ NP\ VP & \qquad S^\circ\ :=\ NP^\circ(VP^\circ) \\
VP & \rightarrow\ V\ NP & \qquad VP^\circ\ :=\ V^\circ(NP^\circ)
\end{array}
$$

We assume a generalized quantifier (Barwise & Cooper, 1981) type analysis of noun phrases.

NP → john, gasoline, my car, a fox   V → is, drinks

The type theory translations of the lexical symbols of the grammar are:

$\text{john}^o := \lambda P.Pj$ 　　　　　　　 $\text{gasoline}^o := \lambda P.Pg$

$\text{mycar}^o := \lambda P.Pc$ 　　　　　　 $\text{a fox}^o := \lambda P.\exists x(\textit{fox } x \wedge Px)$

$\text{a fox}^o_{gen} := \lambda P \forall x(\textit{fox } x \rightarrow Px)$ 　　 $\text{a fox}^o_\pi := \lambda P.(\textit{prty fox } P)$

$\text{is}^o := \lambda P \lambda xP \lambda y(x = y)$ 　　　 $\text{is}^o_\mu := \lambda Q \lambda z \exists P(P z \wedge QP)$

$\text{is}^o_{\mu,\neg tr} := \lambda Q \lambda z \exists P(P z \wedge QP \wedge \neg \forall xPx)$

$\text{drinks}^o := \lambda Q \lambda xQ \lambda y \textit{ drink } y x$

$\text{drinks}^o_\mu := \lambda Q \lambda xQ \lambda y \exists R(R yx \wedge \forall z \forall w(\textit{drink } z w \rightarrow R z w))$

In this grammar we have glossed over the internal complexity of noun phrases. We assume that an indefinite noun phrase such as a fox is ambiguous between an existential, a universal (*gen*; our simplified, quasi-generic), and a prototype (π) interpretation. The copula is is ambiguous between a literal and a nonliteral (μ) interpretation, as is the transitive verb drinks. For good measure, we have added the interpretation of the copula that includes a nontriviality constraint (μ, ¬*tr*) as in Example 9. A minimality constraint (Example 10) can be implemented along the same lines. The reader is invited to check that the grammar maps Example 1 to $\exists x(\textit{for } x \wedge x = j)$, Examples 7, 9, and 11; that is, the grammar generates both literal and nonliteral interpretations. It maps Example 12 to *drink g c* and to Example 14. As it stands, the grammar overgenerates: It combines the generic reading of the object noun phrase with the literal reading of is, and so on. Such readings can be excluded by features in a more detailed encoding of the fragment. In Appendix A we provide a simple Prolog implementation of the grammar and the syntax–semantics interface following Pereira and Shieber (1987), which readers are invited to test.

CONCLUSION

In this article, we have developed an approach to metaphor based on standard type theory (a classical HOL). We capture an asymmetry between metaphor and simile: The literal interpretation of a metaphor comes out as (mostly) false, whereas its nonliteral interpretation is that of a corresponding reduced simile. Our theory captures sense extension in that the property shared between tenor and vehicle includes at least the extension of both. We have presented a compositional syntax–semantics interface, provided a Prolog implementation, and sketched a deductive account of resolution. We discussed how the approach addresses issues of generalization, feature selection, asymmetry, tension, trivialization, prototypicality, truth conditions, comprehension, and generativeness. Summarizing in the form of a slogan, our approach can be said to rescue a weak propositional content of metaphors. To conclude we give our judgment on the commonplace proposition (or metaphor) that classical logic, formal semantics, and metaphors are uneasy bedfellows: False!

ACKNOWLEDGMENTS

Many thanks to Carl Vogel, Tony Veale, Ede Zimmermann, Dick Crouch, David Sinclair, the two sets of anonymous referees for AISB '99 and *Metaphor and Symbol* and John Barnden for stimulating discussion, feedback, and support. Any mistakes are my own. Particular thanks to Deirdre Ní Dheá, who turned the original LaTeX manuscript into a Word document for publication.

REFERENCES

Adams, E. W. (1998). *A primer of probability logic* (CSLI Lecture Notes, No. 68). Stanford, CA: CSLI Publications.

Aristotle. (1952). Rhetoric: Poetics. In W. D. Ross (Ed.), *The works of Aristotle* (Vol. 11). Oxford, England: Clarendon.

Barwise, J., & Cooper, R. (Eds.). (1981). Generalized quantifiers and natural language. *Linguistics and Philosophy, 4,* 159–219.

Black, M. (Ed.). (1962). *Models and metaphors.* Ithaca, NY: Cornell University Press.

Carlson, G., & Pelletier, J. (Eds.). (1995). *The generic book.* Chicago: University of Chicago Press.

Church, A. (Ed.). (1940). A formulation of the simple theory of types. *Journal of Symbolic Logic, 5,* 65–68.

Davidson, D. (1984). What metaphors mean. In D. Davidson (Ed.), *Inquiries into truth and interpretation* (pp. 245–264). Oxford, England: Oxford University Press.

Falkenheiner, B., Forbus, K., & Gentner, D. (1989). Structure-mapping engine. *Artificial Intelligence, 41,* 1–63.

Fitting, M. (1996). *First-order logic and automated theorem proving* (2nd ed.). New York: Springer-Verlag.

Fogelin, R. J. (1988). *Figuratively speaking.* New Haven, CT: Yale University Press.

Gamut, L. T. F. (1991). *Language, logic and meaning, Part 2.* Chicago: Chicago University Press.

Henkin, L. (1950). Completeness in the theory of types. *Journal of Symbolic Logic, 15,* 81–91.

Jaspars, J. (1994). *Calculi for constructive communication: A study of the dynamics of partial states* (ILLC Dissertation Series 1994–4). Amsterdam: Universiteit van Amsterdam, Institute for Logic, Language and Computation.

Montague, R. (1973). The proper treatment of quantification in ordinary English. In J. Hintikka (Ed.), *Approaches to natural language* (pp. 221–242). Dordrecht, The Netherlands: Reidel.

Ortony, A. (1979). Beyond literal similarity. *Psychological Review, 86,* 161–180.

Pereira, F. C. N., & Shieber, S. M. (1987). *Prolog and natural-language analysis* (CSLI Lecture Notes No. 10). Stanford, CA: CSLI Publications.

Thomas, M., & Mareschal, D. (1999). Metaphor as categorisation: A connectionist implementation. In J. Barnden (Ed.), *Proceedings of the AISB '99 Symposium on Metaphor, Artificial Intelligence, and Cognition* (pp. 1–10). Brighton, England: The Society for the Study of Artificial Intelligence and Simulation of Behaviour.

Veale, T., & Keane, M. (1992). Conceptual scaffolding: A spatially founded meaning representation for metaphor comprehension. *Computational Intelligence, 8,* 494–519.

Vogel, C. (2001/this issue). Dynamic semantics for metaphor. *Metaphor and Symbol, 16,* 59–74.

APPENDIX A

```
%% meta.pl  A toy DCG implementation, Josef van Genabith, DCU, CA.
%% implication  %% conjunction  %% negation  %% application
:- op(40,xfy,>).  :- op(30,xfy,&).  :- op(20,fy,~).  :- op(15,yfx,@).
apply(la(X,Y),X,Y).  %% application & reduction (Pereira & Shieber,
   1987)
%%
s(S)  → np(NP), vp(VP),        {apply(NP,VP,S)}.
vp(VP) → v(V), np(NP),         {apply(V,NP,VP)}.
np(la(P,Pj)) → [john],         {apply(P,john,Pj)}.
np(la(P,Pg)) → [gasoline],     {apply(P,gasoline,Pg)}.
np(la(P,Pc)) → [my,car],       {apply(P,car,Pc)}.
%% indefinite, then simplified quasi-generic, then prototype reading
np(la(Q,exists(X, fox(X) & Qx))) → [a,fox], {apply(Q,X,Qx)}.
np(la(Q,forall(X, fox(X) > Qx))) → [a,fox], {apply(Q,X,Qx)}.
np(la(Q,prty(fox,Q)))          → [a,fox].
%% first literal, then metaphorical reading
v(la(P,la(X,Sem)))                → [is], {apply(P,la(Y,X=Y),Sem)}.
v(la(Q,(la(Y,exists(P,P@Y & QP))))) → [is], {apply(Q,la(X,P@X), QP)}.
%% first literal, then metaphorical reading
v(la(Q,la(X,Sem))) → [drinks], {apply(Q,la(Y,drink(X,Y)),Sem)}.
v(la(Q,la(X,Sem))) → [drinks],
{apply(Q,la(Y,exists(R,R@Y@X & forall(Z,forall(W,drink(Z,W) >
   R@W@Z)))),Sem)}.
%%
test :-
  t(N,Sent), s(Sem,Sent,[ ]), write(N), write(':'), write(' '),
    write(Sent), nl, write('Sem:'), write(':'), write(' '),
    write(Sem), nl, nl, fail.
test.
  t(1,[john,is,a,fox]).     t(2,[my,car,drinks,gasoline]).
%%
```

The grammar overgenerates. This can be ruled out in terms of features in a more realistic implementation:

```
| ?- test.
1: [john,is,a,fox]   Sem:: exists(X,fox(X)&(john=X))
1: [john,is,a,fox]   Sem:: forall(X,fox(X)>(john=X))
1: [john,is,a,fox]   Sem:: prty(fox,la(X,john=X))
1: [john,is,a,fox]   Sem:: exists(P,P@john&exists(X,fox(X)&P@X))
1: [john,is,a,fox]   Sem:: exists(P,P@john&forall(X,fox(X)>P@X))
1: [john,is,a,fox]   Sem:: exists(P,P@john&prty(fox,la(X,P@X)))
2: [my,car,drinks,gasoline]   Sem:: drink(car,gasoline)
2: [my,car,drinks,gasoline]   Sem:: exists(P,P@gasoline@car&
                                    forall(X,forall(Y,drink(X,Y)>P@X@Y)))
```

APPENDIX B

To handle Example 16 ("I wrestled with the idea") add the following:

```
np(la(P,Pi)) → [i],        {apply(P,i,Pi)}.
np(la(P,Pi)) → [the,idea], {apply(P,idea,Pi)}.
%% first literal, then metaphorical reading
v(la(Q,la(X,Sem))) → [wrestled,with], {apply(Q,la(Y,wrestle(X,Y)),
  Sem)}.
v(la(Q,la(X,Sem))) → [wrestled,with], {apply(Q,la(Y,exists(R,R@Y@X
  & forall(Z,forall(W,wrestle(Z,W) > R@W@Z)))),Sem)}.
```

The query responses are as expected:

```
3: [i,wrestled,with,the,idea] Sem:: wrestle(i,idea)
3: [i,wrestled,with,the,idea] Sem:: exists(P,P@idea@i&
                                    forall(X,forall(Y,wrestle(X,Y)>P@X@Y)))
```

METAPHOR AND SYMBOL, *16*(1&2), 59–74
Copyright © 2001, Lawrence Erlbaum Associates, Inc.

Dynamic Semantics for Metaphor

Carl Vogel

Department of Computer Science
University of Dublin

An intensional logic with dynamic interpretation is presented to provide a formal semantics for sense extension, lexical ambiguity, and metaphoricity. Intentionality is required to provide the right account of polysemy and homonymy. The dynamics are required to allow the interpretation of a sentence to impact the interpretation of subsequent sentences by adding any extended expressions. Metaphoricity is captured in the classification of indexes at which expressions are evaluated. A mechanism for deciding which predicates to extend is not provided; the intent is rather to demonstrate how dynamic logic can accommodate sense generation and extension. The system is presented, explained, and argued to capture important features of metaphor creation. It provides existential proof of the potential for formal model theoretic semantics to contribute to the theory of metaphor.

Nonliteral language is often thought to be outside the purview of model theoretic semantics. Formal philosophy of language has been influenced by opinions that metaphor, as a form of nonliteral language, is essentially defective or no more than ornamental, even if its use does offer cognitive insights (Percy, 1958). An opposing perspective is that all language use is preconditioned by metaphor, that metaphor is fundamental to cognition and is therefore part of the backdrop to the meaningfulness of sentences rather than something conveyed by them, a view inspired by Lakoff and Johnson (1980). In between is a body of research in artificial intelligence (AI) that analyzes metaphoricity through process models (e.g., Fass, 1991; Veale & Keane, 1992).

Process models of metaphor interpretation in AI research assume that the meaning emerges out of comparisons between domains. Fass (1991), for example, provided a four-way classification of approaches to metaphor: comparison, interaction, selection restriction violation, and convention. However, the compari-

---

Requests for reprints should be sent to Carl Vogel, Department of Computer Science, O'Reilly Institute, Trinity College, University of Dublin, Dublin 2, Ireland. E-mail: vogel@tcd.ie

son approach is present in all of them. Domains are typically encoded as concept hierarchies, and comparisons are measured via structural morphisms. The system of Veale and Keane (1992), for example, identifies substructures that qualify as the reasonable likeness behind the metaphor. Similarly, Fass assumed an overarching taxonomy for all domains and discriminated literal, metaphorical, and anomalous meanings in terms of relative distance in the hierarchy; that is, structural morphisms are identified within subspaces of the single overarching taxonomy. Indurkhya (1994) developed a similar system in which interactionist theories can be explored; in his system, the use of a metaphor can create similarity in domain-type hierarchies.

Models of metaphor understanding devoted to the process of identifying structural preconditions for metaphor do not provide an entire theory of interpretation for nonliteral language: Such a system conveys much about what a metaphorical sentence could mean, but does not offer insight into whether the sentence is true or not. In this article, I focus on the truth conditions of metaphor and the integration of metaphorical expressions with a standard formal framework for the syntax–semantics interface. I do not provide an alternative account of what counts as a good metaphor, nor the relevant analogies or lack of alternative lexical items that give rise to new metaphors. I assume that a suitable account of such can be borrowed from the extensive literature. I assume in this article that meanings must be delivered for metaphorical sentences using the same formal apparatus as the literal senses, albeit with the locus of metaphoricity appropriately identified within the system. A major point is to demonstrate that metaphoricity is not outside the remit of natural language semantics. Rather, explanations of certain aspects of metaphor are integral to the theory of meaning of any sentence in a natural language.

Truth conditions are a small part of meaning, but a profoundly essential part. Without truth conditions, comparison cannot happen: To compare two sets, it is essential to be clear on what comprises the membership criteria for the categories independently, even if the criteria are vague or ill-defined for some compared sets (these criteria are instances of truth conditions). In general, comparing two entities is parasitic on being able to individuate the compared entities, and the degree to which individuation is possible is highly correlated with the capacity to give truth conditions to a sentence asserting an individuation property. This is consistent with psycholinguistic models, such as that of Glucksberg and Keysar (1993), that analyze metaphors as categorization statements; there, as well, everything hinges on the extent to which entities are contained in categories. In overlooking truth conditions, purely structural theories are unable to characterize certain dynamic properties of metaphoricity—for example, that interpreting a metaphor can change the interpreter's concept of the world. (Note that Indurkhya, 1994, did not overlook truth conditions and also recognized dynamic aspects.) Of course, when an interpreter accepts the veracity of a declarative assertion, a sort of change of world is brought about, but this is orthogonal to the kind of change that happens with metaphor. Metaphor brings about a change of possible concepts. It is at the heart of the ontogenesis of literal language. A full theory of metaphor in semantics requires an account of truth conditions inclusive of a theory of the impact on subsequent interpretation.

It may seem that the truth conditions of metaphor are trivial. Metaphors are simply literally false (or, when negated, patently true), whereas their counterparts expressed as similes cannot be false. This is well known, as is the additional fact that a metaphorical assertion can be true or false in its own nonliteral terms.

1. *"Leslie is a library."*
2. *"Leslie is like a library."*

From these issues with truth values, some have concluded that a semantic theory for natural language that relies on a notion of truth will have a hard time articulating a theory of meaning for metaphorical sentences. Davidson (1984), in fact, argued that metaphoricity is indeed a property of language use and hence not the business of semanticists. Certainly, he is not alone in that view (Morgan, 1993).

However, Vogel (1998) argued against the pessimistic extreme of this view and demonstrated that certain aspects of the pragmatics can be captured in a straightforward model-theoretic account, and that account is substantially extended here. Van Genabith (2001/this issue) has provided a type theoretic treatment that analyzes metaphors as reduced similes, with an analysis that differs significantly from a related formal account proposed by Miller (1993). A difference with my proposal is that I agree with Davidson (1984) that metaphor should not be analyzed via translation to simile. The truth conditions differ, and there is not a guarantee of a unique simile to translate a metaphor into, and from which to elide instances of *"like,"* for example, in the nonliteral use of any verb other than the copula. Van Genabith claims that the truth value complementarity between metaphor and simile is mitigated when trivial likeness relations are ignored. This requires, in turn, that the simile (Example 2) be translated into the reduced typicality sentence (Example 3).

3. *"Leslie has a property that is a typical property of libraries."*

Actually, typicality is not essential to his account, but it is the best motivated choice of nontrivial properties to assume. In fact, any nontrivial property will do. The reductionist account by its essential nature omits an important property of metaphor: Similes, even restricted to existentially quantifying over interesting properties, do not have the special force that metaphors do. Glucksberg and Keysar (1993) argued that metaphors are generally perceived as stronger than related similes. They also noticed that a sentence need not have a unique related simile to translate a metaphor into. Although it is technically possible to say that the property shared by tenor and vehicle is the special metaphorical one, such a move undermines the intuitive appeal of the type theory implementation of the comparison approach to a metaphor as if an existential assertion of nontrivial likeness of named categories. Maintaining nontriviality does allow metaphorical statements to be contingent, even on the nonliteral interpretation, but the part of the analysis that captures the nonliteral interpretation does so wrongly in my opinion by equating the metaphor meaning with that of a reduced simile. Metaphors involve (and their first uses create) special senses of the expressions at stake.

Vogel (1998) gave a first-order logical language (see Partee, ter Meulen, & Wall, 1993, for an accessible presentation of foundations of first-order logic) in which literal and nonliteral utterances can be expressed and discriminated. As a first-order account, it allows variables over individuals, but not over relationships between individuals. (The type logic account of van Genabith, 2001/this issue, is one with variables over relations, and hence is not a first-order system.) It is extensional in assuming that any predication is exhaustively specified by providing the set of individuals that stand in the named relation. This means that in a very basic formal system, one that is completely extensional in its analysis of meaning (in that the meaning of a term is fully specified by the set of items that the term truthfully denotes), it is possible to provide an account of metaphoricity in natural language. An advantage of a logical approach such as the one proposed here (or van Genabith's) is in its methodology: We understand completely the syntax and semantics of the language, and therefore we can be fully explicit in stating the theory of metaphor in its terms, as well as how the theory of metaphor integrates with other semantic phenomena.

There are two main ways in which the system of Vogel (1998) diverges from classical uses of first-order logic as a language for meaning representation. First, models for the language initialize each predicate in the language with two characteristic sets rather than one, as is usually the case. One of the characteristic sets is the set of objects that satisfy the predicate literally, and the other set, initially empty, is the set of objects that satisfy the predicate nonliterally. Second, the approach adopts techniques from dynamic semantics (e.g., Groenendijk & Stokhof, 1991). The interpretation of sentences has a dynamic impact on the models. Essentially, certain nonliteral expressions have the capacity to add elements to the characteristic sets of predicates involved in the metaphorical sentence under interpretation. The output of the interpretation of one sentence is the input to the interpretation of subsequent sentences.

This approach correctly discriminates the truth conditions of metaphors and similes without handling them as reduced similes, yet it creates a concrete reason for a related explicit comparison statement to be true. That is, the extensional unpacking of "being the same type as" is for the categories to have an element in common. The account provided by Vogel (1998) allows that a successful metaphor constructs a situation in which two categories do have a common element, and thereafter the comparison sentence is also true. In this framework, the metaphorical expression remains literally false, although it is true with respect to the nonliteral interpretation. Moreover, the approach accommodates the dynamic aspect of meaning in such nonliteral language: Interpreting a nonliteral sentence extends the meaning of predicates at issue by adding nonliterally predicated entities to the corresponding characteristic sets. Thus, the framework provides an analysis of sense extension at the same time. Vogel discussed certain syntactic constraints that seem to be in place to allow or prevent sense extensions from occurring.

However, this model is not rich enough to make all of the required discriminations. In particular, the approach does not allow for there to be more than one way for a predicate to be used nonliterally: Assuming that Example 1 was intended nonliterally, is Leslie being described as knowledgeable or as a lender? This failing is a consequence of the framework's inability to deal with lexical ambiguity in general, even for literal predicates. In this article, I address these problems by recasting the main dynamic interpretation ideas from Vogel (1998) in a more expressive intentional setting. Rather than just a first-order logic, the approach proposed here is a modal predicate logic (see Hughes & Cresswell, 1985, for an overview).

Modal predicate logic derives from the observation that not all logical expressions are truth functional. The specific modalities examined can vary, but typically there is a box operator and a diamond operator. The box operator involves universal quantification over alternatives, and the diamond operator involves existential quantification over alternatives. Thus, necessity would be modeled with the box, and possibility with the diamond, and similarly for other dual modal relations, epistemic, deontic, and so on. The operators are not truth functional in that "possibly p" does not depend for its truth just on the value of p in the real world, but also on alternatives. So, "possibly p" is true if and only if p is true in some accessible alternative, even if p is false in actuality. Axioms appropriate to the modality at stake have underlying constraints on the accessibility relations that connect possible alternatives. The alternatives themselves are modeled as possible worlds, propositions that may be either partial or total in the sense of each predicate being given as true or false in each alternative. At each world we have a set of things, and relations among them, just as in a first-order account. Each world is a way things might have been. It is intensional in acknowledging that predicates are not fully determined by their extensions in the actual world; rather, to understand a predicate is to know its extension, the set of elements it is true of, in each alternative.

In this approach as well, for each predicate, a different possible world provides the characteristic set corresponding to the particular sense at stake. It is not that an entire world is metaphorical or literal, but that a particular world counts as metaphorical for a predicate because of the entities that comprise the predicate at the world. The contrast between literal and nonliteral meaning then is based on the predicate-relative classification of the worlds themselves. A world may be literal relative to some predicate and nonliteral for another. This offers an elegant way of modeling the meaning shift that occurs when a metaphor dies: The sense does not change, but the classification of the sense as literal or nonliteral does. Thus, the interpretation mechanisms for metaphorical expressions are exactly the same as for literal expressions, and estimations of degree of metaphoricity are external classifications of the senses used in the interpretation. The classical modal operators correspond in this framework to quantification over senses: box-$p(q)$ means that $p(q)$ is true (q is p) no matter which of p's senses is considered, and diamond-$p(q)$ means there is some sense of p for which p is true of q. In addition, we can have modal assertions that make explicit reference to a particular sense, rather than using quantification (e.g., *"Leslie is a fox in the cleverness sense of the term"*).

A greater range of potential metaphorical expressions are handled by the current proposal, including individual terms (e.g., names), in addition to predications that take terms as arguments. The system of Vogel (1998) could handle metaphorical uses of Examples 1 and 4.

4. *"Dr. Smith hit her patient with bad news."*
5. *"Einstein here [speaker points] says he knows how to start the grill."*

However, this system did not have a convenient way of handling Example 5, as it did not permit sense extension for constant terms.

Related ideas were discussed by Hintikka and Sandu (1994). They also noticed that the possible worlds semantics for modal logic can be applied to the theory of metaphor and polysemy. They referred to a *meaning line* across possible worlds. This is related to the analysis of identity of individuals in possible worlds semantics for first-order logic. It is standard to assume that at each possible world it is possible to identify counterparts of individuals at other worlds. A meaning line gives a counterpart relation not for individuals, but for predicate names. The meaning line across worlds indicates what entities are in the characteristic set of individuals at each world. The current framework can be seen as giving more concrete detail to a proposal of Hintikka and Sandu, also drawing out further aspects of metaphoricity and polysemy that can be captured in the framework (notably, sense extension) by adding dynamics.

AN INTENSIONAL DYNAMIC SEMANTICS FOR SENSE EXTENSION

The formal presentation of the account is relegated to the Appendix. Here I discuss the main features.

Syntax of the Language

The account presumes that it is possible (but not necessary) to indicate the sense in which an ambiguous expression is intended. It is possible further to indicate whether an expression is used literally or metaphorically. Body language accompanying an utterance can be used for this. Goatly (1997) provided a more exhaustive litany of metaphoricity cues (including explicit use of markers like *metaphorically speaking* and even *literally,* ironically enough). It happens that the cues (apart from *metaphorically*) can be used for other purposes as well; hence, they tend to be ambiguous. However, each can be interpreted by a listener as signaling some sense or other, even if not actually signaling one such. Thus, natural language includes more and less explicit designations of sense. Interpretation, in absence of a signal, is relative to the sense a hearer finds germane.

I assume that senses can be given a partial order. One possible ordering is the frequency relation: the frequency with which the term is used with a particular sense. Another more appropriate to the topic at hand is degree of "liveliness" of a sense, where liveliness corresponds to metaphoricity. Goatly (1997), for example, gave a five-way classification of degrees of conventionalization of metaphor. Death of metaphor is a transformation into literalness, and in the current system this is modeled with rearrangements of the partial ordering of senses.

Designations of sense are quite like the modal operators. Instead of universal or existential quantification over senses, they admit the possibility of referring to a particular way things can be directly. Similar mechanisms are used in modal construals of tense logic (e.g. *"On Wednesday morning, 3 a.m., GMT, November 11, 1965 ... "*); there the alternative worlds are moments in time rather than possible predicate meanings. Indications of sense are assumed to be iterable (also like tense operators: *did want to become* vs. *will want to have been*). I will assume that as with tense, the outermost (in English, the leftmost) designation sets the ultimate reference point.

6. *"In Freud's sense of Marx's sense of 'repression,' economic exploitation is the result of frustrated desires from childhood."*
7. *"In Marx's sense of Freud's sense of 'repression,' frustrated desires from childhood are the result of ownership construals of personal relations."*
8. *"Freud's sense of Marx's sense of 'repression' is the same as/different from Marx's."*

In each case, the designating term is the highest or outermost one in syntactic terms.

In addition to referring to senses, it is also assumed possible to refer deictically. Thus, the language also includes deixis. This is modeled by a function that maps pointing acts to elements of the domain. Deictic acts fix reference, and in idealization I assume that deictic acts are unambiguous. Deixis is also assumed to accompany other referential expressions. It would be possible to allow deictic acts to stand on their own, satisfying argument roles of verbs without other expressions. However, that generality would reduce expository clarity. Thus, deictic acts are seen here as functioning like resumptive pronouns in failing to reduce predicate valency, but distinctly in allowing nonresumptive reference. Like designations of sense, deictic acts are possible in the language, but not necessary. Deixis makes it easy to extend the sense of a name, but is not essential there, nor in extending other nonlogical constants.

A separate axis of interpretation of the language, akin to a listener determining or ascertaining a signal for a sense, is assertional. An utterance can be deemed by an interpreter as new information to be added to world knowledge, or as disputable information. The interpreter will accept new information as an utterance and adapt conceptualization to it. Disputed information is retrieved from utterances not accepted as being new and true. Disputable utterances are tested as true or false. I do not consider information retraction here. The category an utterance falls into along this dimension is patently determined by pragmatic factors. In this analysis, this boils down to how the listener chooses to interpret an utterance. Taking a sentence as assertional involves evaluating it with a dynamic interpretation function; understanding a sentence as up for debate involves evaluating it statically. Any predication, metaphorical or literal, can be a constituent of an utterance that causes a listener to modify beliefs or simply functions as a test. It is up to the interpreter to decide on how to interpret, on the basis of any explicit cues attended to by the listener or simply on the basis of proclivities.

Interpreting the Language

The formal interpretative rules are supplied in the Appendix. The basics out of which the rest is constructed are as follows: There is a set of indexes corresponding to possible worlds (possible senses of predicates). There is also a fixed domain, and an interpretation function that maps individual constants (names) onto elements of the domain, and predicates of arity n onto n place relations constructed from the domain. Each index has a unique identifier. Designations of sense are mapped uniquely to indexes. Each predicate has only one characteristic set at an index, its extension at that index. Deictic acts are interpreted by a function that maps them directly to an element of the domain, much in the way assignment functions interpret variables. Assume that the entire domain is available at each index.

Interpretation of an utterance has an input and an output. The output of interpretation of one utterance is input to the interpretation of subsequent utterances. There are a number of possible ways for a listener to interpret an utterance, depending on whether the listener takes the information as new or disputable. The input and output to interpretation is the domain and interpretation function mentioned earlier.

Assuming the domain is constant for simplicity, what can change over the course of interpretation is precisely the interpretation function—what constants point to what in the domain at an index, what extension a predicate has at an index, what indexes exist.

Take the case of a literal unambiguous expression. It is true at an index if the index is among the literal ones and the entities referred to stand in the mentioned relation. Exactly the same analysis holds for metaphorical expressions, except that the necessary indexes come from a different class of indexes. In fact, the only difference between literal truth and metaphorical truth is whether the relevant senses happen to be classified as such. The forms of evaluation just described are both static. These are used to test the truth values of potentially disputable information. Neither changes the overall state of information. The test of truth amounts to set membership of some entities in the extension of a predicate. The degree of metaphoricity of the sense is a separate issue.

The other possibility is dynamic interpretation. Here also a sense may be indicated, but using dynamic interpretation a new one may be generated, as in the case of absolutely novel metaphor. In this case, the listener has decided to accept the information update supplied by a sentence (literal or nonliteral). The result is simply that a designated individual (in the case of a constant or a unary relation) or a tuple in the general case, is added to the interpretation function. In case the designated index does not yet exist, we have a novel metaphor. In other cases, we have extension of existing senses, literal or nonliteral.

In static interpretation, the input function is the output function. In dynamic interpretation the output function can be distinct (here I consider only possibilities of monotonic increase; however, of course, contraction is an important topic in the belief revision literature). Dynamic interpretation can involve the creation of new indexes or extension of characteristic sets of predicates at existing indexes. Take the latter case first, as it is common to both literal and nonliteral sense extension: Put simply, the characteristic set of the designated predicate at an index is extended to include additional elements. In the case of generating a new sense altogether, the world given as the input to interpretation is taken as the standard. All the denotations of other predicates unrelated to the extended predicate maintain their existing characteristic sets. The extended predicate and any related predicates are stipulated as having in their extension the focused tuple. The result is available for subsequent discourse. The theory does not offer a method for deciding which other predicates to extend, nor does it stipulate a method for identifying which world to extend when the sense is not signaled. Rather, the system is compatible with total ambiguity. It would be quite useful to explore what theoretical approaches to word sense disambiguation dovetail with the proposed approach most naturally.

The framework does not offer an explanation of when to adopt a dynamic interpretation as opposed to a static one. Dynamic interpretation nearly always succeeds when adopted (and even in cases in which the tests involved in static interpretation would have yielded a false result) and sometimes causes a change to the interpretation function. Importantly, static interpretation is not a necessary initial step in the understanding of a metaphor. It is not necessary to interpret a sentence literally first and then metaphorically.

The framework does offer a way to explore the syntax–semantics interface for sense extension of literal and nonliteral expressions. I personally have a hunch that negation is static. That is to say, I believe that the sense of an expression cannot be extended within the scope of negation. This is a very different claim from the possibility of a metaphor being used within the scope of negation.

9. *"Leslie is not a newt."*
10. *"Leslie is not an accountant."*

It seems that new senses cannot be generated under the scope of negation, and further that existing senses cannot be extended in the same environment. This and related constraints can be modeled in the system by stipulating static interpretation for certain logical (and perhaps nonlogical) constants. It is an advantage of the approach that it affords room for such explorations.

DISCUSSION

The interpretation function for nonliteral expressions in general creates a situation in which the expression is nonliterally true, regardless of literal truth values. This system releases the requirement of Vogel (1998) that a prerequisite to extension be the literal falsity of the expression. This means that Example 1 can be simultaneously literally and nonliterally true (provided, for example, that Leslie is literally a library, and also a library in the designated special sense). Interpreting a nonliteral expression with respect to a static interpretation function allows nonliteral expressions to be true or false, with respect to whichever index happens to be the default or signaled index. Sense extension cannot happen using a static interpretation function, but reuse of an extended sense can: Once created, a metaphor can be reused as if literal. This correctly captures the fact that Example 1 can be false, even when used metaphorically, if it is not the case that Leslie is in the characteristic set for the special sense of *"library."* The system also correctly analyzes the first use of a metaphor (subject to certain syntactic restrictions and interpretational decisions) as inescapably (but nonliterally) true.

The difference between literal and nonliteral in this system is not equated with interpretation using a fully static interpretation versus using a dynamic interpretation (see Definition 3 in the Appendix). Rather, it is in the classification of the index at which (either static or dynamic) interpretation occurs. This means that there is no commitment to a strong division between literal and figurative language. There are only senses of terms and classifications of senses. It is up to the individual interpreter to decide what the relative figurativeness ordering is. This classification consists here in grouping the index at which the interpretation for an expression occurs as within $\mathcal{N}$, the set of indexes that are nonliteral for a word, or $\mathcal{L}$, the set of indexes that are literal for a term. Indexes can also be partially ordered to account for the fact that the literal–nonliteral distinction is not binary. The death of metaphor in this system involves nothing but the reclassification of the index at which the metaphorical expression is interpreted as being no longer within $\mathcal{N}$ but $\mathcal{L}$.

In connection with these points, an anonymous reviewer pointed out that some sentences may strike some people as metaphorical and others as completely literal. The reviewer supplied the following example, which demonstrates the interaction of graded categorization with perceptions of metaphoricity.

11. *"Olive oil is nature's most versatile fruit juice."*

I agree completely that the literal–figurative divide is arbitrary, and I hope to have captured that arbitrariness in the model in the simple act of classification of the senses. Any one interpreter will make certain decisions about what counts as a metaphorical sense and what does not. In particular, that senses can be partially ordered by the interpreter captures the graduation of perceived metaphoricity.

Just as the accessibility relations in classical applications of modal logic provide interpretations for modal axioms, here the accessibility relations capture similarities of sense. That is, work on conceptual metaphor can be related to the current proposals by noticing that conceptual metaphors, when expressed in particular sentences, tend to correlate senses of the terms used. It will be interesting to explore the exact properties that different forms of accessibility on sense indexes will have in the interpretation of meaning relations among terms.

Given some expression to interpret at a nonliteral index that extends the characteristic function for the expression at the index, there are likely to be other expressions that also require extension. These ancillary expressions are related to the first through an initial theory of the world.

12. *"Leslie is a fox."*
13. $\forall x \, \text{Fox}(x) \rightarrow \text{Mammal}(x)$
14. $\forall x \, \text{Fox}(x) \rightarrow \text{LikesToStealChickens}(x)$

Given the constituent expressions of Example 12, it is reasonable to imagine that they participate in other sentences that constitute an interpreter's theory of the world, as in Examples 13 and 14. However, imagine the first nonliteral use of Example 12 in which *"fox"* designates a sense corresponding to that of *"sly."* The denotation for *"fox"* at the new sense is structured so that it has Leslie within it. However, it is also reasonable to consider under this same sense whether other predicates connected to fox also require extension to cover Leslie in this new sense. Assuming that Leslie is a human being, a plausible system for deciding which other predicates to extend would leave *"mammal"* untouched (as Leslie is already there literally), but might be inclined to add Leslie to the set of things who like to steal chickens in a nonliteral sense that corresponds to the nonliteral sense of *"fox"* under consideration. Identifying which predicates are pertinent to a metaphor's implicative complex is exactly the business of structural mapping process models. I simply assume that one of them (e.g., Veale & Keane, 1992) can stipulate which additional predicates need to be extended and which ones should be left alone. The current system expects that the other module would deliver in turn each predicate requiring extension, as Definition 3 requires (see Appendix) in general that each extended expression be atomic. Coordination and universal quantification are exceptions, but those just reduce recursively to atomic extensions.

CONCLUSIONS

Nonliteral expressions can be nonliteral because of the predicate or because of the argument. The proposed semantics allows extension from the meaning of both basic predicates and arguments. Extension of the interpretation of a constant can fail if there is not an accompanying deictic act to make clear what the constant is to be extended to, but if deixis is present, a constant can have an extended sense whether used in the scope of a literal predicate or a nonliteral predicate. When used in the scope of a literal predicate, the predication can turn out to be false. However, when used in the scope of a nonliteral predicate, the sentence will evaluate as true and will extend the appropriate sense accordingly. It remains possible to extend each sense to the point of triviality by applying it to all elements of the domain, but if everything is spoken nonliterally then discriminations of meaning are meaningless. The meaning of a metaphorical sentence is not reduced to the meaning of a simile. It creates a reason for a related simile to be true: Nonliteral expressions create an intersection of denotations that thereby licenses a nontrivial likeness between predications involved. Reclassification of indexes as members of $\mathcal{N}$ or $\mathcal{L}$ capture the drift of new metaphorical senses to literalness.

ACKNOWLEDGMENTS

This research is supported in part by Forbairt Basic Research Grant SC–97–623.

I am grateful for enlightening debate on these topics with Josef van Genabith and Tony Veale, and also for extremely useful feedback from various reviewers and editors, especially John Barnden. Many thanks to Deirdre Ní Dheá and Úna Lynch, who saved my metaphorical life.

REFERENCES

Davidson, D. (1984). What metaphors mean. In D. Davidson (Ed.), *Inquiries into truth and interpretation* (pp. 245–264). Oxford, England: Oxford University Press.

Fass, D. (1991). met*: A method for discriminating metonymy and metaphor by computer. *Computational Linguistics, 17,* 49–90.

Glucksberg, S., & Keysar, B. (1993). How metaphors work. In A. Ortony (Ed.), *Metaphor and thought* (2nd ed., pp. 357–400). Cambridge, England: Cambridge University Press.

Goatly, A. (1997). *The language of metaphors,* London: Routledge.

Groenendijk, J., & Stokhof, M. (1991). Dynamic predicate logic. *Linguistics and Philosophy, 14,* 39–100.

Hintikka, J., & Sandu, G. (1994). Metaphor and other kinds of nonliteral meaning. In J. Hintikka (Ed.), *Aspects of metaphor* (pp. 151–187). Dordrecht, The Netherlands: Kluwer.

Hughes, G. E., & Cresswell, M. (1985). *An introduction to modal logic.* London: Methuen.

Indurkhya, B. (1994). Metaphor as a change of representation: An interaction theory of cognition and metaphor. In J. Hintikka (Ed.), *Aspects of metaphor* (pp. 95–150). Dordrecht, The Netherlands: Kluwer.

Lakoff, G., & Johnson, M. (1980). *Metaphors we live by.* Chicago: University of Chicago Press.

Miller, G. (1993). Images and models, similes and metaphors. In A. Ortony (Ed.), *Metaphor and thought* (2nd ed., pp. 357–400). Cambridge, England: Cambridge University Press.

Morgan, J. (1993). Observations on the pragmatics of metaphors. In A. Ortony (Ed.), *Metaphor and thought* (2nd ed., pp. 124–134). Cambridge, England: Cambridge University Press.

Partee, B., ter Meulen, A., & Wall, R. (1993). *Mathematical methods in linguistics.* Dordrecht, The Netherlands: Kluwer.

Percy, W. (1958). Metaphor as a mistake. *Sewanee Review, 66,* 79–99.

van Genabith, J. (2001/this issue). Metaphors, logic, and type theory. *Metaphor and Symbol, 16,* 43–57.

Veale, T., & Keane, M. (1992). Conceptual scaffolding: A spatially founded meaning representation for metaphor comprehension. *Computational Intelligence, 8,* 494–519.

Vogel, C. (1998). A dynamic semantics for novel metaphor. In *Proceedings of the third international conference on information theoretic methods in logic, language and computation* (pp. 116–127). Hsitou, Taiwan: National Science Council.

APPENDIX
AN INTENTIONAL LOGIC FOR SENSE EXTENSION, POLYSEMY, AND METAPHOR

Syntax

Meanings of sentences are represented here by translation into a language that allows (but does not require) exact specification of the sense of a predicate. Explicitness about which is the intended sense also conveys the classification of the sense as literal or nonliteral. There can be a signal of the sense that is used, and if it is present it may be accordingly interpreted; if it is not present, then interpretation will be made relative to a sense determined otherwise. The syntax admits, for example, $c_{m_{m_m}}$ and so on as constants. The potential iteration survives in the semantics.

Definition 1: Syntax

1. Assume a set of constants, C, a supply of variables, V, predicates, $\mathcal{R}$, indications of sense, M, and the usual connectives.
2. If c is a constant and m is an indication of sense, then c_m is a constant.
3. A constant may be accompanied by a deictic act.
4. If P is an n-ary predicate name, $n > 0$, and m is an indication of sense, then P_m is a predicate name.
5. If P is well-formed, then so is $\forall x P$.
6. If P is well-formed, then so is $\neg P$.
7. The usual combination rules with respect to forming predications, complex formulas, and sentences (truth denoting expressions with no unbound variables) apply.

The language provides a basic intentional system that lacks the usual primary focus on interpretations for quantificational modalities. (Modal operators have interesting interpretations, but this is not the issue here.) A predicate has a characteristic set at each world. A predicate may be used in a way that indicates at which world it should be evaluated. The main modal operators of interest are ones that select an explicit index rather than quantifying over indexes. It is further possible for a complex sentence to select one world for one predicate and a different world for a different predicate in the compound. If no sense is indicated for a predicate, interpretation is relative to a particular world. The same is true for constants. *World* and *index* are synonymous mathematical terms here; they carry no ontological baggage. Assume that the same domains are available at each index, but let the interpretation of constants fluctuate. This will account for the interpretations of sentences like Example 1 that use the copula as well as more complicated predications like Examples 4 and 5.

Semantics

Let D be a nonempty domain and W be a set of indexes. The interpretation function I for basic expressions in the language is presented in terms of the tuples comprising it. Assignment functions g map variables to elements of the domain; sense selection functions δ map sense indicators to indexes; and deixis functions d map pointing acts to elements of the domain. Let $\mathcal{L}$ be a subset of W corresponding to the indexes for literal senses, and define $\mathcal{N}$ as $W - \mathcal{L}$.

Definition 2: The Basic Interpretation Function, I

1. $\forall c \in C, w \in \mathcal{L}$ there is a unique $d \in D$: $\langle c, w, d \rangle \in I$.
2. $\forall P^n \in \mathcal{R}, n \geq 0, \forall \tau \in D^n, \langle P, w \rangle \oplus \tau \in I$ iff P is true of the tuple τ at index w.

This specifies the initial interpretation function. When the arity of the predicate (given by a subscript; below arity is indicated only on basic predications, not on possibly compound formulae) is 0, τ is the empty tuple, and P is just a proposition. The symbol $\oplus$ denotes sequence concatenation. The meaning function ($[\![.]\!]$) for arbitrary expressions in L is defined later. This function depends on the interpretation function I, variable assignment g, sense indication s, an index w, and deixis δ. Static or dynamic versions can be called on at indexes given by w or s whether the index is literal or nonliteral. Roughly, static interpretation is a classical special case of the dynamic interpretation clauses given here. Interpretation functions appear to the left and to the right of the meaning function. When interpretation is static, it is exactly the same interpretation function on both sides. With dynamic interpretation, the right-hand side has additional tuples, and the resulting interpretation function becomes the input.

Definition 3: Dynamic Interpretation

1. $I[\![c]\!]^{I \cup \{\langle c,w,\delta(c) \rangle\}, \langle s,g,\delta,w \rangle} = \delta(c)$, iff $\delta(c)$ is defined

2. $I[\![c]\!]^{I, \langle s,g,\delta,w \rangle} = I(c,w)$, iff $\delta(c)$ is not defined but $I(c,w)$ is, and is otherwise undefined.

3. $I[\![c_m]\!]^{I \cup \{\langle c,s(m),\delta(c) \rangle\}, \langle s,g,\delta,w \rangle} = \delta(c)$, iff $\delta(c)$ is defined

4. $I[\![c_m]\!]^{I, \langle s,g,\delta,w \rangle} = I(c,s(m))$, iff $\delta(c)$ is not defined but $I(c,s(m))$ is, and is otherwise undefined.

5. $I[\![x]\!]^{I, \langle s,g,\delta,w \rangle} = g(x), \forall x \in L$

6. $I[\![\langle t^1, \ldots, t^n \rangle]\!]^{O, \langle s,g,\delta,w \rangle} = \langle I[\![t^1]\!]^{O^1, \langle s,g,\delta,w \rangle}, \ldots, O^{n-1} [\![t^n]\!]^{O, \langle s,g,\delta,w \rangle} \rangle$,

7. $I[\![P O]\!]^{I, \langle s,g,\delta,w \rangle} = 1$ iff $\langle P, w \rangle \in I$

8. $I[\![P^n(\sigma)]\!]^{I \cup \{\langle P,w \rangle \oplus^I [\sigma]^{O, \langle s,g,\delta,w \rangle} \} \cup O, \langle s,g,\delta,w \rangle} = 1$ iff $n > 0, |\sigma| = n$

9. $I[\![P_m^n(\sigma)]\!]^{I \cup \{\langle P,s(m) \rangle \oplus^I [\sigma]^{O, \langle s,g,\delta,w \rangle} \} \cup O, \langle s,g,\delta,w \rangle} = 1$ iff $n > 0, |\sigma| = n$

10. $I[\![\neg P]\!]^{I, \langle s,g,\delta,w \rangle} = 1$ iff $I[\![P]\!]^{I, \langle s,g,\delta,w \rangle} = 0$

11. $I[\![P \wedge Q]\!]^{O, \langle s,g,\delta,w \rangle} = 1$ iff $I[\![P]\!]^{M, \langle s,g,\delta,w \rangle} = 1$ and $M[\![Q]\!]^{O, \langle s,g,\delta,w \rangle} = 1$

12. $I[\![\forall x \phi]\!]^{O^U, \langle s,g,\delta,w \rangle} = 1$ iff $O^U = \cup O^i$, where $I[\![\phi]\!]^{O^i, \langle s,g[x/d],\delta,w \rangle} = 1, \forall d \in D$.

Output interpretation functions (e.g., O^i and M) are the smallest ones satisfying the conditions.

Definition 3, Points 1 through 4 handle nonliteral constants: Either it is a first and deictic use, or it is a reuse of a previously extended sense. The first use is the case of sense extension—the interpretation function that is the output of interpretation has an additional tuple in it, the content of which depends on deictic reference (Points 1 and 3). This is at the heart of what was referred to earlier when mentioning that interpreting a new metaphor changes the interpreter's concept of the world: A new sense exists with referents, and this sense is available to interpretation of subsequent discourse. Subsequent use of the same extended sense may apply it to the same individuals (Points 1–4) or to additional elements of the domain (Points 1 and 3). If deixis is not given, then it can only be a subsequent use of the sense-extended constant, and is thus static with respect to the interpretation function, whether or not the sense is indicated (Point 2 vs. Point 4). The interpretation of variables is unaffected by polysemy (Point 5). The interpretation of a sequence of constants and variables is sequential, and the output of the interpretation of each term in the sequence is the input to the interpretation of the next one (Point 6). This echoes the widely assumed asymmetry of argument structure in natural languages. Senses may be signaled or not for any of the terms, as in the absence of a sense indication, interpretation is relative to the designated index w. Propositions are not given a dynamic interpretation (Point 7). Points 8 and 9 allow the sense of a predicate name to be extended. In Point 8 the sense is extended at a nonliteral index independently specified, and in Point 9 it is relative to an indicated sense. Note that the output interpretation function includes additions made in the interpretation of the predicate's argument. Negation (Point 10) has a static interpretation, but conjunction is dynamic (Point 11); the second conjunct of an expression can be interpreted relative to the extended interpretation from the first conjunct. This means that the second conjunct can be a literal predication of arguments with a nonliteral meaning created by prior discourse. Finally, universal quantification (Point 12) extends meaning by iterating over all elements in the domain in combinations of the preceding possible ways of extending meaning. That the intermediate interpretation functions in Points 11 and 12 are the minimal ones that work means that arbitrary choices will not do, only recursively constructed extensions of the initial interpretation. This definition of the meaning function, [.], is just one of the possible specifications an interpreter can make use of. Another is fully static.

METAPHOR AND SYMBOL, *16*(1&2), 75–86
Copyright © 2001, Lawrence Erlbaum Associates, Inc.

The Continuum of Metaphor Processing

Heather Bortfeld

Department of Cognitive and Linguistic Sciences
Brown University

Matthew S. McGlone

Department of Psychology
Lafayette College

We describe the explanatory value of a relativistic account of metaphor processing in which different modes of metaphor interpretation are assumed to be operative in different discourse contexts. Employing the cognitive psychological notion of a processing set, we explain why people might favor attributional interpretations of figurative expressions in some circumstances and analogical interpretations in others. Applying this logic to findings in the psycholinguistic literature on metaphor suggests that some of the competing models may in fact describe different points on a continuum of metaphor processing.

In his classic essay "When Is Art?" Goodman (1978) argued that philosophical efforts to describe the attributes unique to art objects (i.e., what is art) might be misguided. Instead, he argued that the term *art* does not describe a class of objects that is intrinsically different from other object classes, but rather the product of interpreting an object in a particular way under particular circumstances. Our goal in this article is to point out the explanatory value of this benign form of philosophical relativism in developing a comprehensive cognitive theory of metaphor understanding. Just as the aesthetic status of an object can vary from context to context, so too can the meaning of a metaphor. A comprehensive theory of metaphor must be able to account for the fact that metaphors can be and often are interpreted in fundamentally different ways in different circumstances. Although some theorists have acknowledged that context plays a significant role in the time course of metaphor in-

Requests for reprints should be sent to Heather Bortfeld, Department of Cognitive and Linguistic Sciences, Box 1978, Brown University, Providence, RI 02912. E-mail: Heather_Bortfeld@brown.edu

terpretation (e.g., Gibbs, 1980; Ortony, Schallert, Reynolds, & Antos, 1978), there have been few, if any, attempts to explore the role of context in the manner with which metaphors are interpreted and ultimately are the products of the interpretation process. We argue that investigative efforts of this sort are not only warranted on empirical grounds, but also offer the added benefit of resolving long-standing disputes among various metaphor theorists.

THE PROCESS INVARIANCE ASSUMPTION

Research on metaphor in cognitive science has typically focused on the conceptual processes underlying metaphor comprehension. Two general classes of process models have emerged from this research. *Attributional models* (e.g., Glucksberg, McGlone, & Manfredi, 1997) characterize metaphor comprehension (e.g., *"Our love has been a rollercoaster ride"*) as a search for properties (e.g., exciting, scary, full of ups and downs, etc.) of the vehicle concept (*"rollercoaster ride"*) that can plausibly be attributed to the topic (*"our love"*). In contrast, *domain-mapping models* (e.g., Gentner & Clement, 1988) characterize metaphors as conveying a common relational structure between the topic and vehicle concepts (e.g., the lovers correspond to travelers, their relationship corresponds to the rollercoaster car, their excitement corresponds to the speed of the car, etc.). Noting that certain domain mappings underlie a variety of conventional figurative expressions (e.g., the mappings between *"love"* and *"journeys"*), some theorists have posited the existence of conventional conceptual metaphors that provide the conceptual basis for our understanding of the vast majority of metaphorical expressions (Gibbs, 1994; Lakoff, 1987).

Not surprisingly, there has been much debate among theorists about which model offers the most parsimonious or veridical account of how people comprehend metaphors in text and conversation (Bortfeld, 1998, 2000; Gibbs, 1992; Glucksberg, Keysar, & McGlone, 1992; McGlone, 1996; see also Murphy, 1997). The disputes over theoretical differences stem in part from a tacit assumption of process invariance common to both classes of models. This assumption holds that metaphor comprehension derives from a single conceptual process (whether it be attribution or domain mapping) that is consistently applied by all interpreters in all contexts in which metaphors are encountered. This pervasive assumption has not been challenged because the vast majority of empirical studies on metaphor comprehension have relied on indirect comprehension measures (e.g., the time it takes readers to comprehend metaphors), rather than examination of the products of comprehension (i.e., people's written or oral interpretations of metaphor meaning).

The handful of empirical studies that have focused on the products of metaphor comprehension have found considerable interpretive variability as a function of interpreter characteristics (age, knowledge state, and interpretive goal), contextual characteristics (whether the metaphor is presented in isolation or ongoing discourse), and statement characteristics (whether the metaphor is conventional or novel, relatively apt or inapt, etc.; Blasko & Connine, 1993; Bortfeld, 1998, 2000; Gentner & Clement, 1988; McGlone, 1996; Tourangeau & Rips, 1991). The fact that people's interpretations of a given metaphor may vary does not necessarily indicate that they are products of different interpretation processes. For example, the difference between interpreting *"Matt is a pig"* as meaning Matt is gluttonous or Matt is slovenly might reflect nothing more than the differential salience of pigs' stereotypical properties in different contexts. In this case, it is plausible that the different interpretations are derived by choosing differentially salient pig properties via the same property selection process.

However, other cases of interpretive variability suggest that people can use qualitatively different kinds of vehicle information to characterize the topic. For example, consider the different ways one might interpret *"A lifetime is a day"* (McGlone, 1996). A day is a relatively short span of time, and consequently one might interpret the statement as an assertion that life is short. Alternatively, one might recognize a day as comprised of stages that thematically correspond to periods in life, and thereby interpret the statement as an assertion that dawn corresponds to birth, morning to childhood, noon to middle age, and so on. Like the interpretations of *"Matt is a pig"* discussed earlier, the former interpretation involves using a stereotypical property of the vehicle concept *"day"* to characterize the topic *"lifetime."* Such an interpretation is predicted by attributional models; that is, the vehicle is understood as being emblematic of a category of short time spans that can plausibly contain the topic (Glucksberg et al., 1997). In contrast, the latter interpretation involves using a system of relations in the vehicle to characterize the topic. This rich, analogical interpretation is predicted by domain-mapping models; that is, people search for epistemic correspondences between entities in the topic and vehicle conceptual domains (e.g., Lakoff, 1987). Both interpretations are plausible, and one cannot be deemed more apt than the other without the benefit of contextual support. After all, context ultimately determines what meaning people will derive (Gerrig & Bortfeld, 1999). However, the assumption that metaphor interpretation derives from a single conceptual process prevents both the attributive categorization and domain-mapping models from accounting for alternative interpretations.

ATTRIBUTIONAL VERSUS RELATIONAL METAPHORS

Metaphors such as *"A lifetime is a day"* occupy an intermediate position in a similarity space between what Gentner and Clement (1988) referred to as attributional metaphors and relational metaphors (see Figure 1). Attributional metaphors such as *"Matt is a pig"* highlight the common attributes (e.g., gluttonous, slovenly, untidy,

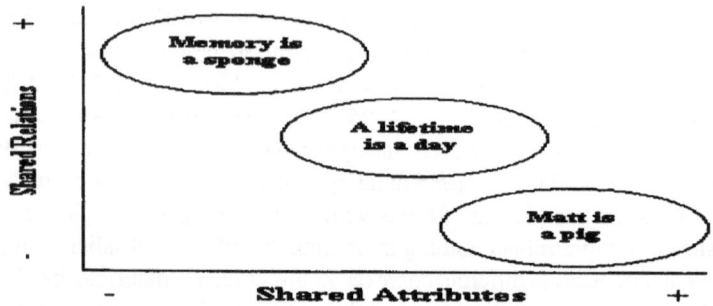

FIGURE 1   Metaphors depicted in a Shared Relation × Shared Attribute similarity space.

etc.) of topic and vehicle concepts that do not have obvious analogical similarities. In contrast, relational metaphors such as *"Memory is a sponge"* convey common analogical structures (e.g., information is to memory as water is to a sponge) in topic and vehicle concepts that do not have obvious attributional similarities. For the remainder of this discussion, we use the term *analogical* rather than Gentner and Clement's *relational* because it best characterizes the differences between the two types of metaphor.[1] In between attributional and analogical metaphors are those like *"A lifetime is a day,"* which can be interpreted in terms of the topic and ve-hicle common attributes (e.g., short time span) or analogical conceptual structures (e.g., birth = dawn, childhood = morning, etc.). Proponents of attributional and do-main-mapping models of metaphor have differentially sampled metaphors from the semantic similarity space on which to focus their theoretic efforts.

Glucksberg and his colleagues formulated their attributional model primarily to de-scribe how people interpret metaphors in conversation (Glucksberg & Keysar, 1990; Glucksberg & McGlone, 1999; McGlone, 1996). Because of the time constraints im-posed by the obligation to participate in an ongoing conversational exchange, conver-sational metaphors tend to be fairly simple in nature, highlighting a few attributes that are relevant to the point being made (e.g., *"My job is a jail," "My ex-wife's lawyer is a shark,"* etc.). In contrast, Gentner and her colleagues (e.g., Gentner & Clement, 1988) account for metaphors in a domain-mapping framework that was originally formu-lated to explain meaning-rich, scientific analogies. Such analogies (e.g., *"An atom is like the solar system"*) are almost purely analogical in nature, and most of the example

---

[1]Holyoak and Nisbett (1987) criticized Gentner's (1983) analytic distinction between attribute and relational similarities on the grounds that the latter were representationally reducible to the former. Nonetheless, Holyoak and Nisbett also suggested that an analytic distinction can be drawn between lit-eral comparisons (based on property matches) and analogies (based on schematic structural matches). Our use of the term *analogical metaphors* to describe what Gentner referred to as relational metaphors reflects our appreciation of the dispute over attributes and relations, still suggesting that there are simi-larities between concepts that transcend mere attributes.

metaphors (e.g., *"A cigarette is a time bomb"*) used to illustrate the domain-mapping model are from the relational portion of Gentner and Clement's (1988) similarity space. In a similar vein, Lakoff and his colleagues (e.g., Lakoff, 1987; Lakoff & Turner, 1989) focused primarily on clusters of idiomatic expressions that imply epistemic relations between domains (e.g., *"blow your stack," "get hot under the collar,"* and *"do a slow burn"* all imply analogical relations between the domains of anger and heated fluid under pressure).

This selective sampling of examples from the diverse corpus of metaphorical expressions explains in part why metaphor theorists have tacitly embraced the process invariance assumption. Within the limited set of metaphorical expressions that attributional and domain-mapping theorists have chosen to focus on, such an assumption is unnecessary: It is theoretically plausible that attributional metaphors are understood via a single conceptual process and analogical metaphors are understood via a single, albeit different conceptual process. There is no pressing theoretical need to question process invariance unless one tries to account for the interpretation of attributional and analogical metaphors within the same model. In this respect, the variability with which people interpret hybrid metaphors such as *"A lifetime is a day"* suggests that the labels attributional and analogical are not exclusively descriptive of metaphor classes, but also of different modes of metaphor processing. In some circumstances, people may interpret the metaphor in attributional mode (life is short), and in others they interpret it in an analogical mode (dawn = birth, morning = childhood, etc.).

METAPHOR PROCESSING SETS?

The notion of a processing mode or set has a long history in cognitive psychology. In the domain of problem solving, the observed bias of participants to apply rules to new problems that facilitated solving previous problems—even when these rules offer a suboptimal strategy for addressing the new problem—is characterized as a processing set (Lovett, 1998; cf. Luchins, 1942). The processing set notion has also proved useful in describing persistent language interpretation strategies as well (Bobrow & Bell, 1973; Carey, Mehler, & Bever, 1969; Garrett, 1969; Mackay, 1969; Marshall, 1965). For example, Carey et al. (1969) demonstrated that establishing a set to interpret particular syntactic structures can bias the way people interpret literally ambiguous sentences. They presented a literally ambiguous sentence following several unambiguous sentences that had the same grammatical structure as one of the meanings of the ambiguous sentence. Participants modally perceived the meaning of the ambiguous sentence in terms of the set structure. For example, when sentences such as *"They are unearthing diamonds"* and *"They are installing benches"* preceded the ambiguous sentence *"They are visiting sailors,"* participants modally interpreted *visiting* in the last sentence as a progressive transitive verb. However, when this sentence was preceded by *"They are incoming signals"* and *"They are emerging nations,"* *visiting* was modally interpreted as a gerundive adjective (see also Mackay, 1969).

Similarly, it has been shown that presenting people with supplemental semantic information can induce a processing set that can bias people's interpretations of polysemous words. In a dichotic listening paradigm, Garrett (1969) presented ambiguous sentences such as *"The fans were noisy that night"* to the attended ear while simultaneously presenting unambiguous sentences such as *"Baseball spectators were yelling"* to the unattended ear. She found that people tended to understand the ambiguous sentence in a manner consistent with the unambiguous prime. In this case, people were more likely to interpret *fans* as referring to people rather than mechanical devices.

Bobrow and Bell (1973) invoked the notion of a processing set to describe the way people interpret idiomatic expressions. They reasoned that our comprehension of idioms such as *"let the cat out of the bag"* proceeds as if the idiomatic phrase were effectively a long word. Processing the phrase as a long word differs from that for literal phrases, wherein each word is perceived, meanings are retrieved from semantic memory, and then each meaning is mapped into a representation of the phrase's overall meaning (Quillian, 1968). To empirically investigate the dichotomy of literal and idiomatic modes of processing phrases, Bobrow and Bell presented people with sets of five sentences, the fifth of which included a phrase that could be interpreted literally or idiomatically (e.g., *"John gave Mary the slip"*). In the literal set condition, the preceding four sentences were sentences that could be interpreted only literally, (e.g., *"Alan fed biscuits to his dog"*). In the idiomatic set condition, the preceding sentences all contained idioms (e.g., *"Henry was in hot water"*). Consistent with previous demonstrations of processing set effects, people were more likely to recognize the literal meaning of *"John gave Mary the slip"* (i.e., John gave an undergarment to Mary) first when it was preceded by literal sentences, but were more likely to recognize its idiomatic meaning first (John evaded Mary's pursuit) when it was preceded by idiomatic sentences. Bobrow and Bell interpreted this finding as evidence that people are inclined to interpret idioms as long words when this processing mode is induced by prior context. Although there are intrinsic problems with conceiving idioms as merely long words (see McGlone, Glucksberg, & Cacciari, 1994), the notion of distinct literal and idiomatic processing modes has nonetheless been supported by many contemporary studies of idiom comprehension (Cacciari & Tabossi, 1988; Gibbs, 1980; Swinney & Cutler, 1979).

For our purposes, the notion of different processing sets may be used to account for a significant portion of the observed variability in metaphor interpretation: Qualitatively different interpretations may be the product of different metaphor processing sets. By this logic, the attributional and domain-mapping models can be viewed not as competing comprehensive models of metaphor interpretation, but rather as descriptions of distinct processing sets that are activated in different interpretational contexts. The models' status as distinct processing accounts has not heretofore been acknowledged because researchers have chosen to focus on metaphors from the extreme ends of the attributional–analogical similarity continuum. Thus, attributional and analogical interpretations are likely to be preferred for metaphors that are predominantly (if not exclusively) attributional (e.g., *"Clouds are marshmallows"*) or analogical (e.g., *"Sarcasm is a veil"*) in nature. The processing set account is most clearly evident when one examines people's interpretations of metaphors that afford both attributional and analogical interpretations and manipulates the contexts in which these hybrid metaphors appear.

As a preliminary test of the processing set account of metaphor interpretation, we developed a variation of the set paradigm used by Bobrow and Bell (1973). Twenty-four Lafayette College undergraduates generated written interpretations of target hybrid metaphors after interpreting a block of context metaphors constructed to induce an attributional or analogical processing set. To induce an attributional set, participants interpreted a series of four predominantly attributional metaphors prior to interpreting the target. In the same manner, an analogical processing set was induced when participants interpreted a series of predominantly analogical metaphors prior to the target. An example set of context and target metaphor materials is presented in Table 1. For any given target metaphor, participants saw only one set of the context sentences (attributional or analogical). The metaphors used to construct these materials were drawn from sets used by Gentner and Clement (1988), McGlone and Manfredi (in press), and Ortony, Vondruska, Foss, and Jones (1985). Classification of each metaphor as attributional, analogical, or a hybrid was made on the basis of a pretest using procedures described by Gentner and Clement (1988).

To measure the efficacy of the processing set manipulation, two independent judges (2 additional Lafayette College undergraduates) evaluated the number of references that were made to attributional and analogical topic–vehicle commonalities in the experimental participants' written target metaphor interpretations. Judges were trained to classify as an attributional commonality any description of a physical property shared by the topic and vehicle concepts; descriptions of a common system of attribute correspondences (independent of the attributes them-

TABLE 1
Examples of the Context and Target Sentences Used to Investigate
Metaphor Processing Sets

Attributional Context Metaphors	Analogical Context Metaphors
"Jellybeans are balloons."	*"Smiles are magnets."*
"The sun is an orange."	*"Sarcasm is a veil."*
"Soap suds are whipped cream."	*"Crime is a cancer."*
"Some roads are snakes."	*"Salesmen are bulldozers."*

selves) were classified as analogical commonalities. For example, an interpretation of *"Tree trunks are drinking straws"* as meaning that tree trunks are long and tube-shaped was classified as attributional; in contrast, the meaning that tree trunks pull water up like a drinking straw does was classified as analogical. The trained judges were blind to the processing set condition in which a given interpretation of a target metaphor was generated.

Inspection of participants' written interpretations revealed a pattern similar to that observed in previous processing set studies. When hybrid targets were preceded by attributional metaphors, attributional topic–vehicle commonalities were mentioned first in 66.6% of participants' interpretations. When the target was preceded by analogical metaphors, analogical commonalities were mentioned first in 83.3% of the interpretations. These results suggest that participants were initially sensitive to topic–vehicle commonalities in the target that were of the same kind as those in the preceding context metaphors. However, it was not the case that processing set blinded participants to plausible interpretations that were not of the sort favored by the induced set. Overall, participants generated both attributional and analogical interpretations for hybrid metaphors 70.8% of the time. Thus, the processing set manipulation exerted its influence primarily on the order with which attributional and analogical commonalities were mentioned, but did not block one sort of interpretation in favor of another. Both sorts of interpretation are available, by definition, in a hybrid attributional–analogical metaphor; the processing set manipulation merely influenced the degree to which the different types of commonalities were accessible.

AVAILABILITY VERSUS ACCESS

The distinction between the accessibility and availability of conceptual information in metaphor interpretation figures prominently in disputes over the potential role that conceptual metaphors might play in figurative language comprehension. This debate is also relevant to the proposal we present here, that different modes of metaphor interpretation are operative in different discourse contexts. Depending on the context in which a hybrid metaphor is used, either its attributional or its analogical characteristics may be more appropriate. A question stemming from this is whether one or the other characteristic will already have been recognized and be accessed or whether only the appropriate context induces such recognition. A more detailed discussion of the difference between availability and access will illustrate our point.

Lakoff and his colleagues (Lakoff, 1987; Lakoff & Turner, 1989) argued that conceptual metaphors underlie our use and understanding of conventional figurative expressions in a variety of domains. For example, consider the different metaphors that are reflected by idioms we use to describe anger. One conceptual metaphor for anger is that of heated fluid under pressure. Idioms that seem to reflect this conceptual metaphor include *"flip your lid," "let off steam,"* and *"blow your top."* An alternative conceptual metaphor for anger is that of animal-like behavior, reflected in idioms such as *"bite someone's head off"* or *"hopping mad."* Although broad conceptual metaphors seem to motivate many idiomatic expressions (Gibbs, 1994), their analogical role in idiom use and comprehension is questionable. When people encounter an idiom such as *"blow your top"* in text or conversation, is the *"ANGER IS HEATED FLUID UNDER PRESSURE"* metaphor merely available, or, as Lakoff (1990) argued, automatically accessed? A conceptual structure is available if it is simply represented in a given language user's semantic memory (Miller & Johnson-Laird, 1976). Although many theorists have raised serious doubts about whether conceptual metaphors are so represented (Jackendoff & Aaron, 1991; McGlone, 1996; Murphy, 1997), we stipulate that they are for the discussion here. The availability of a conceptual structure is, by definition, context independent: It is either stored in semantic memory or it is not. In contrast, access to a conceptual structure that participates in language comprehension is typically context dependent: It may be retrieved in certain contexts but not others (e.g., Anderson & Ortony, 1975).

What determines whether a conceptual metaphor will be accessed to guide idiom comprehension, as opposed to being merely available (albeit dormant) in semantic memory? One important factor is the operative time constraints in the circumstances under which an idiom is encountered. The normal pace of conversation would seem too fast for interlocutors to retrieve the entire conceptual metaphorical underpinnings of a phrase like *"blow your top"* (Glucksberg, Brown, & McGlone, 1993). From a functional standpoint, it is not clear that there is any utility to retrieving a complex metaphorical structure when merely retrieving the phrase's relevant import (i.e., someone got really angry) would suffice (Glucksberg et al., 1993). As with most words, the comprehension of idioms may functionally proceed in many contexts without recourse to or awareness of their etymological origins.

However, there are clearly some contexts in which retrieval of a figurative expression's metaphorical underpinnings is functional. For example, when one is reflecting on why he or she thinks an idiom means what it means (e.g., a language teacher describing how to use an idiom appropriately or, conversely, a student explaining to a language teacher why he or she thinks an idiom means what it means), it would be quite functional to retrieve as much of its underlying metaphorical structure as possible. Bortfeld (1998) demonstrated that, in such circumstances, there is a surprising degree of consistency in people's accounts of their understanding of an idiom's metaphorical derivations, even among non-native speakers who have just learned an idiom from a new language. For example, when asked about their understanding of the idiom *"blow your top,"* both native and non-native speakers report mental images of containers about the size of one's head bursting open and spouting their contents upward, as opposed to envisaging someone expelling air at a spinning child's toy. This evidence suggests that the conceptual correspondences comprising the metaphor

"ANGER IS HEATED FLUID UNDER PRESSURE" may very well be represented in semantic memory and thus are available for retrieval in interpretational circumstances that are conducive to reflection.

A very different sort of reflective context in which conceptual metaphorical information is likely to be accessed is that of someone reading prose for pleasure or an analytic purpose. In these cases, both the lack of time constraints and the motivation to make intertextual connections are conducive to the reader retrieving and using conceptual metaphorical information. Interpreting metaphorical language in this context as opposed to how one does this in a typical conversation parallels the distinction Gerrig and Healy (1983) drew between metaphor appreciation and comprehension. They argued that although both types of metaphor processing may potentially draw from the same knowledge base, the representation of metaphor meaning in comprehension is a truncated version of that created during appreciation. A truncated representation is perfectly functional when the goal is merely to comprehend a metaphor; in contrast, an appreciative assessment of the metaphor (e.g., judging whether it is relatively apt or inapt) requires a richer representation. Gerrig and Healy's demonstration that differences in metaphor aptness (e.g., *"Drops of molten silver filled the night sky"* is highly apt, whereas *"Drops of molten resin filled the night sky"* is less so) do not translate into differences in comprehension time is consistent with the claim that appreciation and comprehension constitute distinct modes of metaphor processing.

CONCLUSION

Our survey of psychological research on metaphor interpretation leads us to two conclusions. First, the manner in which figurative expressions are interpreted is only partially determined by their linguistic structure. Although in some extreme cases metaphors may be classified as purely attributional or analogical in nature, there are many that constitute hybrids of these species. How these hybrid metaphors are interpreted depends not only on conceptual representations available in semantic memory, but also the processing set that is active when the expression is interpreted. Analogously, the availability of an underlying conceptual metaphor for understanding a conventional figurative expression does not necessitate retrieval of this conceptual information in all contexts in which the expression is encountered. Whether the interpreter will employ a conceptual metaphor processing set depends critically on the operative time constraints in the interpretational context, as well as on the goals of the interpreter.

Second, the dispute over which process model constitutes the definitive processing account of metaphor interpretation may simply be a red herring. Just as our interpretations of a given literal phrase structure or polysemous word can be dramatically influenced by processing sets, so might our interpretations of metaphorical language from context to context and goal to goal. In this regard, metaphor theorists should distinguish between cases in which there is a legitimate conflict between models and other cases in which the models describe different points on a continuum.

REFERENCES

Anderson, R., & Ortony, A. (1975). On putting apples into bottles. A problem of polysemy. *Cognitive Psychology, 7,* 167–180.

Blasko, D., & Connine, C. (1993). Effects of familiarity and aptness on metaphor processing. *Journal of Experimental Psychology: Learning, Memory, and Cognition, 19,* 295–308.

Bobrow, D., & Bell, S. (1973). On catching on to idiomatic expressions. *Memory & Cognition, 1,* 343–346.

Bortfeld, H. (1998). A cross-linguistic analysis of idiom comprehension by native and non-native speakers. *Dissertation Abstracts International: Section-B: Sciences and Engineering, 59,* 0432.

Bortfeld, H. (2000). *A cross-linguistic analysis of idiom comprehension.* Unpublished manuscript, Brown University, Providence, RI.

Cacciari, C., & Tabossi, P. (1988). The comprehension of idioms. *Journal of Memory and Language, 27,* 668–683.

Carey, P., Mehler, J., & Bever, T. (1969). When do we compute all the interpretations of an ambiguous sentence? In W. Levelt & G. Flores D'Arcais (Eds.), *Advances in psycholinguistics* (pp. 61–75). Amsterdam: North-Holland.

Garrett, M. (1969). Does ambiguity complicate the perception of sentences? In W. Levelt & G. Flores D'Arcais (Eds.), *Advances in psycholinguistics* (pp. 48–60). Amsterdam: North-Holland.

Gentner, D. (1983). Structure-mapping: A theoretical framework for analogy. *Cognitive Science, 7,* 155–170.

Gentner, D., & Clement, C. (1988). Evidence for relational selectivity in the interpretation of analogy and metaphor. In G. Bower (Ed.), *The psychology of learning and motivation* (pp. 307–358). San Diego, CA: Academic.

Gerrig, R., & Bortfeld, H. (1999). Sense creation in and out of discourse contexts. *Journal of Memory and Language, 41,* 457–468.

Gerrig, R., & Healy, A. (1983). Dual processes in metaphor understanding: Comprehension and appreciation. *Journal of Experimental Psychology: Learning, Memory, & Cognition, 9,* 667–675.

Gibbs, R. (1980). Spilling the beans on understanding and memory for idioms in context. *Memory & Cognition, 8,* 149–156.

Gibbs, R. (1992). Categorization and metaphor understanding. *Psychological Review, 99,* 572–577.

Gibbs, R. (1994). *The poetics of mind.* Cambridge, England: Cambridge University Press.

Goodman, N. (1978). When is art? In *Ways of worldmaking* (pp. 53–74). Indianapolis, IN: Hackett.

Glucksberg, S., Brown, M. E., & McGlone, M. S. (1993). Conceptual analogies are not automatically accessed during idiom comprehension. *Memory & Cognition, 21,* 711–719.

Glucksberg, S., & Keysar, B. (1990). Understanding metaphorical comparisons: Beyond similarity. *Psychological Review, 97,* 3–18.

Glucksberg, S., Keysar, B., & McGlone, M. S. (1992). Metaphor understanding and accessing conceptual schema: Reply to Gibbs. *Psychological Review, 99,* 578–581.

Glucksberg, S., & McGlone, M. S. (1999). When love is not a journey: What metaphors mean. *Journal of Pragmatics, 31,* 1541–1558.

Glucksberg, S., McGlone, M. S., & Manfredi, D. (1997). Property attribution in metaphor comprehension. *Journal of Memory and Language, 36,* 50–67.

Holyoak, K., & Nisbett, R. (1987). Induction. In R. Sternberg & E. Smith (Eds.), *The psychology of human thinking* (pp. 50–91). New York: Cambridge University Press.

Jackendoff, R., & Aaron, D. (1991). Review of "More than cool reason." *Language, 67*, 320–328.

Lakoff, G. (1987). *Women, fire, and dangerous things: What categories reveal about the mind.* Chicago: University of Chicago Press.

Lakoff, G. (1990). The invariance hypothesis: Is abstract reason based on image schemas? *Cognitive Linguistics, 1*, 39–74.

Lakoff, G., & Turner, M. (1989). *More than cool reason: A field guide to poetic metaphor.* Chicago: University of Chicago Press.

Lovett, M. (1998). Choice. In J. Anderson & C. Lebiere (Eds.), *The atomic components of thought* (pp. 255–296). Mahwah, NJ: Lawrence Erlbaum Associates, Inc.

Luchins, A. (1942). Mechanization in problem solving. *Psychological Monographs, 54*(6, Whole No. 248).

Mackay, D. (1969). Mental diplopia: Towards a model of speech perception at the semantic level. In W. Levelt & G. Flores D'Arcais (Eds.), *Advances in psycholinguistics* (pp. 76–100). Amsterdam: North-Holland.

Marshall, J. (1965). Syntactic analysis as a part of understanding. *Bulletin of the British Psychological Society, 18*, 28.

McGlone, M. S. (1996). Conceptual metaphors and figurative language interpretation: Food for thought? *Journal of Memory and Language, 35*, 544–565.

McGlone, M. S., Glucksberg, S., & Cacciari, C. (1994). Semantic productivity and idiom comprehension. *Discourse Processes, 19*, 167–190.

McGlone, M. S., & Manfredi, D. (in press). Topic–vehicle interaction in metaphor comprehension. *Memory & Cognition.*

Miller, G., & Johnson-Laird, P. (1976). *Language and perception.* Cambridge, MA: Harvard University Press.

Murphy, G. L. (1997). Reasons to doubt the present evidence for metaphoric representation. *Cognition, 62*, 99–108.

Ortony, A., Schallert, D., Reynolds, R., & Antos, S. (1978). Interpreting metaphors and idioms: Some effects of context on comprehension. *Journal of Verbal Learning and Verbal Behavior, 17*, 465–477.

Ortony, A., Vondruska, R. J., Foss, M. A., & Jones, L. E. (1985). Salience, similes and the asymmetry of similarity. *Journal of Memory and Language, 24*, 569–594.

Quillian, M. R. (1968). Semantic memory. In M. Minsky (Ed.), *Semantic information processing* (pp. 227–270). Cambridge, MA: MIT Press.

Swinney, D., & Cutler, A. (1979). The access and processing of idiomatic expressions. *Journal of Verbal Learning and Verbal Behavior, 18*, 523–544.

Tourangeau, R., & Rips, L. (1991). Interpreting and evaluating metaphors. *Journal of Memory and Language, 30*, 452–472.

METAPHOR AND SYMBOL, *16*(1&2), 87–108

Processing Unfamiliar Metaphors in a Self-Paced Reading Task

Frank Brisard, Steven Frisson, and Dominiek Sandra

Department of Germanic Languages
University of Antwerp

In 2 self-paced reading experiments, we investigate the processing characteristics of unfamiliar metaphorical subject–predicate structures. The literal first hypothesis predicts that processing metaphorical expressions of the type *"an x is a y"* will proceed more slowly than in the case of literal statements of the same type. This prediction is confirmed: At the position of the metaphorical term, reaction times were indeed higher for the metaphorical conditions than for the literal ones. This result was obtained both without (Experiment 1) and with a supportive context sentence (Experiment 2). In Experiment 2, a distinction also emerges between apt and nonapt instances, such that reaction times for apt metaphors are no longer significantly higher toward the end of the clause containing them. This suggests that, when embedded in a rich context, the interpretation of unfamiliar apt metaphors can be completed by the end of a fragment that can serve as a clause.

The model that has probably had the strongest effect on the literature concerning the time course involved in processing metaphorical language starts from the so-called *literal first hypothesis,* which observes that the interpretation of metaphors needs to pass through a stage in which the literal meaning of an utterance is processed before its figurative meaning can be computed. The hypothesis is derived from a *stage model* of metaphor comprehension that originated in contemporary philosophy of language. In their semantic theories, scholars like Searle (1979) and Grice (1975) distinguished between sentence meaning and utterance or speaker's meaning, reflecting the distinction between what is said through an utterance (i.e., the conventional, literal meanings of words and how they are syntactically combined) and the ulterior meaning the speaker wishes to express, which can only be

---

Requests for reprints should be sent to Frank Brisard, Department of Germanic Languages, University of Antwerp–UFSIA, Prinsstraat 13, 2000 Antwerp, Belgium. E-mail: frank.brisard@ua.ac.be

implicated in the case of metaphor. According to this model, language users encountering metaphorical statements first determine the sentence meaning, then discover that this meaning cannot be what the speaker intended (because it is typically false, literally), only to reject the literal meaning afterward in favor of a derived, contextually computed figurative meaning. Strictly speaking, this model also implies that the search for a figurative interpretation cannot be initiated if a literal interpretation is successfully integrated in the sentence context. That is, any type of literal (sentence) meaning that can be ascribed to an utterance and that is in some way compatible with the interpretive context in which the utterance appears will automatically block the process of finding an alternative reading. Thus, the position of literal meaning in this model is clearly an absolute one and always prevails on nonliteral derivations, whether of a metaphorical nature or otherwise related to the computation of the speaker's meaning.

In the original formulations of the literal first hypothesis, a figurative interpretation can only be computed at the end of a sentence. In what follows, however, we adopt a version of the model that is more in line with current theories of incremental processing. To verify the claims of literal first as a stage model, the hypothesis is put forward that, if a metaphorical meaning is derived from a previously determined literal one, metaphors must take longer to process than (matched) literal propositions. To test this, it is necessary to tap the processing of metaphors online (i.e., during the word-for-word presentation of the metaphorical stimulus sentence). If reaction times (RTs) are measured for complete metaphorical sentences only, other components of metaphorical interpretation, like the actual appreciation of the metaphor in question (Gibbs, 1992), will have already had the chance to exert an influence on the course of processing. A genuine online measuring technique, then, can be implemented effectively with experimental stimuli that are limited to the fairly simple structure of categorization statements, like "An X is a Y," because the position of the literal and metaphorical term Y remains constant in such expressions (in contrast with referring metaphors, where this type of positional variation is much harder to control for). Now, instances of metaphorical language, especially when they are of the predicative type distinguished here, invite language users to make classifications that do not fit any literal taxonomy. Thus, metaphor is a device that enables the language user to redeploy a category scheme that characterizes one domain to effect a reorganization of another. If somebody says "Friends are trees," he or she is asking us to consider that some items are not only people but also trees, a taxonomic error, unless of course only the relevant similarities are sorted out. Theoretically, this sorting and the resulting nonliteral interpretation need not occur after a literal interpretation is attempted. But how could this be empirically demonstrated?

Many experiments have been carried out with exactly the type of predicative stimuli included in the present series. Fairly few of these studies, however, address the issue of unfamiliar metaphors, among them Blasko and Connine (1993) and

Gerrig (1989). Glucksberg, Gildea, and Bookin (1982) used predicative sentence structures to investigate whether the literal meaning of a metaphorical expression can be responded to before its metaphorical meaning is available. In the experiment, participants had to decide whether sentences were literally false or not; that is, they had to monitor for the literal meaning of the sentence only and react to that. RTs and error rates were compared between two categories of literally false items: metaphors and nonmetaphorical false statements. The authors demonstrated that it is more difficult for participants in a speeded response task to answer "no" to sentences like *"All jobs are jails"* (as opposed to blatantly false sentences without a possible metaphorical interpretation), with longer RTs and higher error rates. This shows that the availability of a true metaphorical meaning interferes with the execution of a negative response. However, as the authors themselves remarked, these findings cannot really reject the literal first hypothesis. The construction of the metaphorical meaning in a second stage may be so fast and automatic as to interfere with the processing of the literal meaning regardless of its secondary status. Alternatively, participants may simply be unable to monitor for early processing stages, as these may be part of the processing machinery of a modular system (which by definition cannot be penetrated by conscious attention processes). Hence, although Glucksberg and associates reported findings that seem to argue against a literal first model, the nature of the experimental tasks employed does not make the interpretation of their data compelling in this respect. The only thing these experiments show is that metaphor processing is highly automatic; it cannot be brought under the conscious control of participants (to facilitate task compliance), yet they remain neutral as to the involvement of metaphorical meanings in an initial stage of processing.

The interpretive ambiguity in Glucksberg et al. (1982) derives from the fact that they used an indirect method to compare literal and metaphorical processing by focusing on the processing of the literal meanings of metaphorical statements. Indeed, the indirectness of comparisons between literal and metaphorical conditions constitutes one of the more important difficulties in the interpretation of experimental results concerning the time course of metaphor comprehension. A second methodological problem in experimental studies of metaphor is exemplified in Gibbs's repeated attempts to falsify literal first. Concretely, Gibbs questioned the psychological validity of the literal first hypothesis on the basis of experimental work on indirect requests, idioms, and sarcastic utterances (for overviews, see Gibbs, 1984, 1994). Gibbs also referred to experimental work of his own in which he showed that these kinds of expression (which can be subsumed, together with metaphors, under the general heading of figurative language) are processed as fast as literal sentences. However, the experimental paradigms reported by Gibbs may not be the best way to assess literal first, as global RTs measured for complete sentences, as the standard technique applied in these experiments, cannot tease apart immediate from additional processing.

In sum, if there is research indicating that literal and figurative meanings may be processed equally fast, the methodology that is generally used does not allow us to conclude that this is due to the use of an identical processing routine (a single stage for both types of language use) or, for that matter, to the parallel activation of two different routines (one for literal and one for figurative language). In particular, when experimental paradigms do not employ a genuine online method to measure RTs within sentences (word-for-word measurements), small effects may simply be undetectable. Consequently, when measuring global RTs (for complete sentences), the presence of an effect does not allow its exact localization (i.e., where it begins to emerge and how long it persists), and its absence (the null effect) may be due to the fact that the effect has been drowned in the sum of all individual word RTs. To make statements on the processing routine itself, one must therefore track the course of interpretation more meticulously, as also argued by Dascal (1989). This is what can be achieved by using a self-paced reading task. We ran two experiments in which this technique was applied.

Only unfamiliar metaphors are investigated, because they provide the most obvious point of entry for an investigation into the creative function of figurative language and its online characteristics. Much of the existing experimental literature on the interpretation and processing of figurative language either does not systematically control for the distinction between conventional and novel metaphors in the design of the stimuli, making the reported results hard to interpret, or explicitly chooses to concentrate on (more or less highly) conventionalized instances. However, the chances of finding effects that would confirm the literal first model in the processing of conventional metaphors will be considerably lower given that the meanings involved are likely to be represented in the mental lexicon, in which case factors (like frequency and saliency; cf. Giora, 1997) enter the picture that do not strictly take part in the frame proposed by literal first. This is a theoretical problem for literal first, but not one that should prevent us from seeing the model as generating general predictions that hold for both types of metaphor, conventional and new. The decision to focus on unconventional metaphors in this series of experiments is a strategic one, in that it should enable us to examine the processing behavior of meanings that are, by definition, not represented in the lexicon and that can therefore not be affected by such extra variables.

GENERAL METHOD

In the experiments reported here, we make a direct comparison between the RTs of metaphorical and literal expressions. We create the best possible matching between material types, as we use the same predicative structures (with differing subjects) for literal and metaphorical conditions. To achieve better online accuracy, we also make use of a technique, self-paced reading, that stays close to the language user's real-time processing behavior. In a self-paced reading experiment, the reader has to move gradually through a sentence at his or her own pace. A timing device measures the time during which each word within a stimulus sentence remains on the computer screen.

The purpose of these experiments is (a) to study differences and similarities in the online (word-for-word) processing of literal and metaphorical sentences and (b) to do so over two different conditions: with supportive preceding context (providing the ground for the subsequent metaphors and a comparably suitable context for the literal sentences) and with no preceding context. The second concern is also included in the design of the experiments because it has been experimentally demonstrated that a preceding context with a strong supportive value for metaphorical readings will generally facilitate the comprehension of metaphors. In the experiments, literal and metaphorical sentences are of the categorization type *"An x is a y,"* followed by additional linguistic material (relative clause, prepositional phrase, etc.) modifying the category name *y*. Thus, for each target word two sentences are produced that are identical from the predicate slot onward (up until the end of the sentence), differing only in the kinds of subject assigned to the predicate. This differentiation in subject assignment, then, is the sole factor distinguishing between a literal and a metaphorical reading of the resulting categorization statement.

Literal: *"An oak is a tree ... "*
Metaphorical: *"A friend is a tree ... "*

Within the set of literal sentences, a further distinction is made between prototypical and peripheral members of the category at issue (e.g., for tree, *oak* would be prototypical and *maple* peripheral). For metaphorical sentences, we differentiate between apt and nonapt metaphors—that is, between sentence types in which the assignment of a metaphorical subject will result in metaphors of a fairly high quality and those in which this is not the case. With respect to metaphor aptness, a number of cross-modal priming experiments (Blasko & Connine, 1993) have shown that metaphors of low familiarity (the type considered here) do not trigger figurative meanings unless the metaphors in question have been rated highly or moderately apt (i.e., of high or moderate quality). That is, aptness seems to play a role in processes of comprehension when participants are faced with metaphorical statements they have not encountered before. Again, however, the specific locus of the reported effects turns out to be highly volatile and cannot be pinned down on lexical activation patterns for the topic or vehicle of the metaphor. In fact, the authors themselves suggested that the construction of figurative meanings for these metaphors was caused by a set of emergent properties for each metaphorical phrase. The present experimental paradigm, which makes use of self-paced reading, is particularly well suited to deal with issues such as these, as the possibilities for locating the source of effects for figurative meanings follow automatically from applying a technique that records RTs for each individual word of a stimulus sentence (and not just for topics or vehicles).

When measured on the category name y in a self-paced reading task, targets appearing in literal sentences should, on the whole, be read faster than those that occur in metaphorical sentences. This is motivated by the contention, within the literal first hypothesis, that literal meanings need to be (at least partially) processed before a figurative one can start being computed at all. For the experiments reported here, this means that the problematic category status of metaphorical targets needs to be established first. Only then can participants begin to look for possible alternative interpretations (which they typically have to do if they are to understand the meaning of the sentence as a whole). In addition, we predict that differences in RTs on the predicate position of literal sentences will also reflect the degree of membership that can be attributed to the subjects of these sentences, so that targets (e.g., *tree*) will be read more slowly when preceded by peripheral members (e.g., *maple*) than when they appear in sentences containing prototypical subjects (e.g., *oak*). This particular prediction should fall out of the standard results reported in the prototype literature. For unconventional metaphors, the latter qualification relates not so much to the status of the subject as a category member (because no actual membership is assumed in these metaphorical statements), but rather to their contribution to the aptness of the resulting metaphor. Thus, the prototypical versus peripheral status of category members in literal statements is complemented by the distinction in aptness between two types of metaphorical statement. Targets in nonapt metaphors should be read more slowly than those in apt ones, because aptness determines the ease of comprehension for unconventional metaphors.

EXPERIMENT 1

Method

Materials and design.   The items in the experiment gave rise to four conditions, presenting two literal and two metaphorical terms per category name. They were selected on the basis of several pretests. Participants throughout the pretests and the experiments were native speakers of Dutch, and the sentences presented to them were in Dutch. No participants were used twice.

In Pretest 1 (see Table 1), a production task featuring 51 category names, participants had to write down, for each category, as many members as they could within a limited period of time (20 min on average, although individual participants who could not finish the task in time were allowed to complete the questionnaire within an additional 5 min). The category labels were distributed over three lists of 17 items. Each of these lists was presented in two random orders to 20 participants (i.e., there were 60 participants in total). On this basis, 24 semantic categories,

TABLE 1
Pretest 1: Selected Category Names With Prototypical and Peripheral Items

Category	Prototype	Positions 1 + 2	Peripheral
Monster	Dragon [10]	70%	Werewolf [2]
Amusement park (Dutch: *pretpark*)	Walibi [20]	79%	Phantasialand [3]
Insect	Fly [19]	89%	Beetle [2]
Flower	Rose [20]	85%	Carnation [2]
Tree	Oak [16]	69%	Maple [2]
Artist	Painter [11]	50%	Poet [2]
House	Villa [17]	73%	Farm [2]
Color	Red [17]	88%	Violet [2]
Genius	Einstein [16]	65%	Edison [2]
Organ	Liver [19]	100%	Pancreas [2]
Medication (Dutch: *medicijn*)	Aspirin [11]	63%	Penicillin [2]
Bird	Sparrow [18]	55%	Owl [2]

Note. The number of tokens generated for each listed category member is indicated in square brackets. Percentages indicating the relative frequencies of prototypical items mentioned in first and second position are included in the third column.

each with its prototypical and peripheral members, could be selected for further use in the experiments.

Only categories for which participants produced more than 10 members were considered. Prototypical items were selected on the basis of their absolute production frequencies (they had to occur at least 10 times; i.e., half of the participants should have mentioned them), as well as a weighted frequency that favored first and second mentions. Peripheral category members, although obviously showing a very low production frequency, had to be mentioned by more than one participant. Concretely, all but one of the selected peripheral category members were mentioned each time by exactly two participants.

An overview of the results obtained for the following two pretests is provided in Table 2, each time limited to those items that have been retained on the basis of earlier selection procedures.

In Pretest 2, we focused on metaphorical combinations with the purpose of discriminating between apt and nonapt terms. To each of the remaining 24 categories, six nonmember terms were added as subjects in a subject–predicate structure of the type "*An x is a y.*" Thus, 144 unfamiliar metaphors were created, distributed over three lists of 48 items (with each predicate or category name appearing not more than twice per list). With two random orders per list, a total of 60 participants had to assess the quality of the metaphorical subject–predicate relation on a 7-point scale ranging from 1 (*nonapt*) to 7 (*apt*). A second group of 60 participants was asked to judge the conventionality of these metaphors on a 7-point scale, as we are only interested in metaphors with a fairly low degree of conventionality and familiarity. As can

TABLE 2
Mean Ratings and Standard Deviations for Selected Items in Pretests 2 and 3

| | Pretest 2 | | | |
| | Aptness | | Conventionality | |
Rating Level	M	SD	M	SD
High	4.50	.70	3.66	1.08
Low	1.76	.23	1.53	.34

| | Pretest 3 | |
| | Aptness | |
Rating Level	M	SD
High	3.72	1.18
Low	3.18	1.27

be gathered from the first section in Table 2, we obtained reliable differences between two sets of metaphorical items, which were called apt and nonapt, respectively. In addition, all metaphors scored around or below average for conventionality (i.e., they were generally considered fairly unconventional). When considering the mean rating scores of the items that got selected, aptness and conventionality were highly correlated ($r^2 = .84, p < .001$). On the basis of these results, the 12 categories appearing in Table 1 were selected, each of them giving rise to two metaphors. Only metaphorical items with a low degree of conventionality were marked for selection, and the aptness distinction was distributed equally over these items, so that each category produced one apt and one nonapt metaphor.

The participants in Pretest 3 had to assess the quality of the metaphors remaining from the previous pretest. This time, however, full sentences were presented, consisting of a categorization statement (*"An x is a y"*) plus additional material following the target (e.g., *"A friend is a tree with very firm roots and thick branches"*). Each stimulus was rated by 6 participants. Here, the rating distance dividing apt and nonapt metaphors proved to be smaller than in the previous pretest. This indicates that in an offline task, the addition of lexical material elaborating the ground of the presented metaphors affects their interpretability. We expect such an effect of interpretation to show up again in online tasks toward the end of the stimulus sentence—that is, by measuring RTs on target words that occur fairly late in the course of processing (cf. the Results section). When analyzing the two mean scores for aptness, taken together over Pretests 2 and 3, a highly significant effect was obtained, $F_i(1, 11) = 75.42, p < .001$. Also, the interaction between conditions with and without additional lexical material (the difference between Pretest 2 and

3) and aptness turned out significant, $F_i(1, 11) = 71.75, p < .001$, which indicates that there is a significant effect of aptness between the stimulus types presented in the two pretests; that is, bad metaphors occurring in full-blown sentences (not just bare subject–predicate structures) are generally considered more apt.

Finally, Pretest 4 investigated, for the same 12 categories, whether the contrast in their literal counterparts between the selected prototypical and peripheral items was large enough to be measurable in an RT experiment. To check this, we ran a verification task of the type performed by McCloskey and Glucksberg (1979), using counterbalanced lists. (The experiment was run over 2 nonconsecutive days.) Eight participants had to verify under time pressure whether the prime, the first item presented (during 1 sec), was a member of the category whose name was given immediately afterward (the target). The results showed that the literal prototypical items, as derived from Pretest 1, were indeed verified more rapidly than the peripheral ones (with significant differences in subject and item analyses, both $ps < .05$). This allowed us to use these two (literal) item sets in the actual experiments with their status as prototypical or peripheral category members empirically verified.

In sum, 12 category names were selected, each giving rise to four different conditions depending on the status of the subject term (examples are translated from Dutch):

- Literal and prototypical: *"An oak is a tree with very firm roots and thick branches."*
- Literal and peripheral: *"A maple is a tree with very firm roots and thick branches."*
- Metaphorical and apt: *"A friend is a tree with very firm roots and thick branches."*
- Metaphorical and nonapt: *"A racist is a tree with very firm roots and thick branches."*

Considering the way the materials have been constructed, they constitute 12 sets of matched quartets. Additional filler material was created with sentences that had the same initial structure (*"An x is a y"*) as the critical items. Of these fillers (24 in total), half were metaphorical in the sense of not providing an established categorization of the grammatical subject. The other half presented literal statements. In turn, half of the metaphorical fillers were considered apt metaphors (as established on the basis of extra material used in Pretest 2), whereas the other half yielded nonapt items. For literal sentences, half of the filler set presented prototypical members and the other half contained peripheral ones. Neither literal nor metaphorical filler items were analyzed in the experiments, as they had not been subjected to Pretests 3 or 4, respectively.

All of the critical items were distributed over four lists, with each of the lists yielding two randomized orders. To each list, the same filler items were added. The critical items were distributed across the lists according to the following criteria: Each list contained all of the 12 category names (no one category appeared twice in a list), with three instances of each of the four types distinguished earlier. There were 15 participants per list ($N = 60$).

Procedure.   Before the experiment started, participants were instructed, orally and in writing, about relevant aspects of the experimental procedure. During the experiment, they were sitting in front of a computer screen in a darkened room. The experimental sentences appeared on the screen one by one. For each sentence, a number of dashes represented the words contained in that sentence without revealing the actual words themselves beforehand. Participants could thus assess the length of the sentences without anticipating the exact nature of their contents. The participants' task was to proceed through the sentence one word at a time, making use of the middle button on a button box. Each time this button was pressed, a new word would appear (and the previous one would disappear). Participants were told to go through the entire sentence this way, maintaining a reasonable reading speed and making sure they saw and understood each of the words making up the sentence. The time-out for individual words was set at 2 sec.

After the sentence was read, the same question always appeared ("Do you agree with this statement?"). At that point, participants had to indicate their answer by pressing the left or right button on a button box. This question was inserted to ensure that participants were motivated to attend to the content of the sentences instead of to their formal characteristics. They were asked to answer the question in a fully personal and subjective way, stressing the focus on content even more. All of the filler and experimental sentences were designed so that their contents made for more or less informative, nontrivial statements, making the task varied enough to hold the participants' attention.

Each experiment contained two pauses of 10 sec, which participants could abort if they wanted to proceed faster.

Participants.   For Experiment 1, 60 undergraduate foreign-language students volunteered to participate. Nobody participated more than once. All students were native speakers of Dutch. No volunteers were paid for their participation.

Results.   Average RTs were calculated on the target word (i.e., the category name *y,* which is the point in the sentence where its literal or metaphorical status becomes clear) and on the following word (target + 1) to check for spillover effects. The results for target + 1 are not reported here, as they completely match those for the target word itself. RTs were also measured on target2 and on target2

+ 1. The second target occurs at the syntactic end of a clause. It indicates the first point in the sentence following the actual target at which a complete grammatical clause can be construed (in the example *"An X is a tree with very firm roots and thick branches,"* target2 will coincide with the word *roots*). This second target thus indicates the point at which participants have enough sentential material to wrap up their interpretation of (part of) the proposition. It is experimentally demonstrated (as discussed in Frazier, 1999; see also Abrams & Bever, 1969) that additional processing can be assumed to go on at this particular point in the processing of a sentence. For the metaphorical statements, this means that something of a stable metaphorical interpretation becomes available due to the sufficient amount of (incrementally processed) preceding information. Therefore, in case metaphorical sentences of the present type cause participants to put their interpretation on hold until more material is available for interpretation, result patterns for target2 should differ from those for the first target. In addition, RTs on the word immediately following this second target (*and* in the preceding example) are recorded to check whether the additional processing occurring on target2 spills over to the following region target2 + 1. Target2 + 1 is always a function word, a grammatical expression that adds little or no lexical information to the proposition at issue. In the experiments reported here, this position is typically filled by simple conjunctions (*and, but*), relative pronouns, or prepositions. Given the lexically impoverished nature of this class, it is to be expected that processing properties for such words will show little or no significant variation.

In discussing the results for this and the following experiment, we perform analyses of variance (ANOVAs) by subjects and items. These tests indicate the probability that subjects (or some related procedure) and items can be treated as random effects. If a level of statistical significance is reached, it will be implied that the results obtained are justifiably generalizable over subjects or stimulus materials; that is, the probability of their random nature is negligible. For by-subjects analyses, this means that the sample subjected to the experiment is representative of an entire population (typically to be interpreted as the average native speaker). For by-items analyses, the failure to find a significant effect would suggest that an effect is restricted to (part of) the set of materials used in the experiment; that is, this set is not representative of the experimental topic at hand. In the latter case, it is likely that the items that produce an effect have some properties that the experimenter has not noticed.

Table 3 shows the RTs for the four conditions in Experiment 1 on target, target2, and target2 + 1. An ANOVA for a 2 (sense: literal or metaphorical) × 2 (quality: prototypical–peripheral and apt–nonapt) design was performed on the RTs of target words. On the first target word, literal sentences were read significantly faster than their metaphorical counterparts, resulting in an overall sense effect for the subject and the item analysis, $F_s(1, 59) = 6.20, p < .05; F_i(1, 11) = 6.60, p < .05$. Pairwise analyses between and within conditions only indicate significant differences be-

TABLE 3
Experiment 1: Mean Reaction Times (Msec) and Standard Deviations on Target,
Target2, and Target2 + 1

Condition	Target (= Category Name)		Target2		Target2 + 1	
	M	SD	M	SD	M	SD
Literal, prototype	514	212	564	238	525	169
Literal, peripheral	476	168	607	280	491	126
Metaphor, apt	554	248	631	327	518	176
Metaphor, nonapt	545	244	650	305	539	162

tween the literal–peripheral condition and the two metaphorical conditions (both ps < .05). The comparisons between literal–prototypical and the two metaphorical conditions are not significant (both ps > .08).

On target2, the overall sense effect between literal and metaphorical sentences remains for the subject analysis, $F_s(1, 59) = 4.71$, $p < .05$, and is marginal in the item analysis, $F_i(1, 11) = 3.76$, $p < .08$. At this point in the processing of the sentence, the prototypical condition stands out as the fastest one by about 40 msec, when compared to the literal peripheral condition (as opposed to the 31 msec in the opposite direction on target). Still, no significance can be found between them, $F_s(1, 59) = 1.89$, $p > .1$; $F_i < 1$. The aptness distinction was nonsignificant on this position as well (both $Fs < 1$). Pairwise analyses between conditions only yield significance for comparisons between literal–prototypical and the two metaphorical conditions: prototypical versus apt, $F_s(1, 59) = 4.57$, $p < .05$; $F_i(1, 11) = 2.30$, $p > .1$; prototypical versus nonapt, $F_s(1, 59) = 7.51$, $p < .01$; $F_i(1, 11) = 3.78$, $p < .08$. The two other comparisons are nonsignificant (both $ps > .11$).

No sense effect was found on target2 + 1, $F_s(1, 59) = 1.84$, $p > .1$; $F_i < 1$. All pairwise analyses yield nonsignificant effects (all $ps > .1$), except the by-subject comparison between literal–peripheral versus nonapt metaphors, $F_s(1, 59) = 5.31$, $p < .05$; $F_i(1, 11) = 2.27$, $p > .15$. The absence of a sense effect here, and the fact that this is the main point of distinction with respect to the preceding data points, suggest that our selection of target2 as a point of syntactic closure is well motivated. It might be argued that no differences between metaphorical and literal conditions surfaced at this point because of a possible floor effect. However, given the observed effects reported for the same position in the following experiment, this seems very unlikely.

In general, Experiment 1 shows that it takes longer to process the same set of words when a predicate assignment is interpreted metaphorically than when it is interpreted literally. This may not be all too surprising, of course, as participants in the experiment received no preceding context sentence. They may have been slow on the metaphors simply because they missed the relevant information to make the intended metaphorical interpretation. From this perspective, Experiment 1 can be considered a benchmark for Experiment 2, which introduced a context motivating in advance the sentence that followed it, whether metaphorical or literal. In the following experiment, we also pay particular attention to the absence of an overall sense effect that was found on target2 + 1 in Experiment 1.

EXPERIMENT 2

Method

Materials and design.   The experimental materials and design were the same as those in Experiment 1. Each sentence was now preceded by a context sentence. Items in this experiment were of the following type.

Example 1
Context:
"Great deeds don't need large audiences."
Target:
"A painter/poet/spider/bear is an artist [target] who lives on his talents [target2], in silence."

Example 2
Context:
"The smallest seed can grow into something big."
Target:
"A(n) oak/maple/friend/racist is a tree [target] with very firm roots [target2] and thick branches."

The context sentences were the same for literal and metaphorical conditions. They had been carefully selected on the basis of pretests. In one pretest, participants had to choose between two possible context sentences on the basis of considerations of semantic integration. These context sentences preceded all four conditions distinguished in the experiments (literal: prototypical vs. peripheral; metaphorical: apt vs. nonapt), as equally distributed over different lists; that is, with each list containing the same number of sentences for each of these conditions. In another pretest, participants had to assess the degree of semantic congruity between context and target sentences on a 7-point scale ranging from 1 (*low integration*) to 7 (*high integration*). In both pretests, although critical items were obviously preceded by meaningful context sentences, half of the filler items followed nonsense context sentences (i.e., grammatical sentences unrelated to the topic of the target sentences), included to counterbalance the high degree of semantic integration for appropriate context sentences. The four conditions were matched on contextual fit.

In the experiment, the relation between a target sentence and its preceding context is such that one or several words appearing in the target belong to the same domain as, or are otherwise semantically linked to (part of), the content evoked in the context. For instance, the word *artist* is closely related to the word *audiences* in the target sentence (and even more so in the original Dutch example, which made use of an expression, *publiek,* that typically occurs in the context of artistic stage productions). Any possibility of interpreting other words in the target sentence as themselves metaphorical (in addition to the dominant metaphor elaborated by the target sentence) was excluded, except if such terms appeared after the final data point, target2. When preceding metaphorical target sentences, the context sentence is seen here as providing the ground for the metaphorical interpretation of the target, because it is supposed to motivate the particular similarities that are evoked by the metaphorical description. This is usually done by simply highlighting one of the more salient properties of the so-called vehicle, which can be done directly (e.g., *trees* grow from small *seeds*) or through inference (e.g., an *artist* shows or performs his or her work in relation to an *audience*).

The context sentences presented in this experiment are limited compared to the use of more elaborate preceding context in other, similar experiments. Again, this is a strategic consideration, in that finding effects (or the absence thereof) that would differ from the ones in Experiment 1 (i.e., obtaining an effect of context) with such a small context will constitute harder proof of the influence of a preceding context on metaphor comprehension. Previous research (Inhoff, Lima, & Carroll, 1984; Ortony, Schallert, Reynolds, & Antos, 1978) has shown that, typically, a preceding context needs to be fairly long (in any case, longer than the 4- to 10-word range given as short context by Inhoff et al., 1984) for metaphorical interpretations to be available as fast as literal ones. However, it should be pointed out in this respect that the context used in these studies did not systematically exploit a (conceptual) relation between its own content and that of the metaphorical target sentence, in contrast to the context type employed in the present experiment. In fact, Inhoff et al. (1984) correctly pointed out that metaphorical sentences following the type of context used by Ortony et al. (1978) behaved similarly to literal sentences preceded by semantically unrelated (literal) contexts, which shows that the processing problems involved were not necessarily due to the distinction between literal and figurative conditions, but rather to issues of conceptual integration and what might be called discourse coherence (on a local scale). In contrast, when contexts were used that did contain metaphorically interpretable elements, RTs for metaphorical sentences dropped considerably. In a similar vein, Gildea and Glucksberg's (1983) search for a minimal appropriate context leading to immediate metaphor comprehension suggests that preceding context sentences, if they are to facilitate metaphor comprehension, should at least contain references to (salient) properties of the metaphorical vehicle (here and in Gildea & Glucksberg's case, the sentence predicate). Again, this is true for the context sentences that were used in this experiment as well. As a consequence, the length of the preceding context, when appropriately constructed, is of secondary importance. What is important is the interaction between length and content; the preceding context should be long enough to allow participants to construe a workable ground for the interpretation of the metaphor that is to follow.

Procedure.   The procedure for Experiment 2 was the same as that for Experiment 1, except that a context sentence preceded each target sentence. The entire context sentence appeared on the screen at once (i.e., no self-paced reading was required for this part of the materials). Having read this context sentence, participants pushed the middle button on a button box to make the sentence disappear, at which time they could proceed with the actual target sentence in the manner described for Experiment 1. This time, the time-out for individual words in the target sentences was set at 2.5 sec. Because target sentences were preceded by context, we had to grant a minimal amount of extra reading time to allow participants to successfully integrate the lexical content of each word with this previous information. Also, given the higher processing load placed on participants because of the inclusion of context material, we wanted to make sure that not too many time-outs occurred that would be due to effects of fatigue.

Participants.   In Experiment 2, 60 undergraduate foreign-language and business students volunteered. Nobody participated more than once in any of the pretests. All students were native speakers of Dutch. No volunteers were paid for their participation.

Results.   Figure 1 compares results from Experiment 2 with those from Experiment 1, for the target position.

Globally, all RTs are much shorter than those in Experiment 1 (a difference of about 100 msec on average). As in Experiment 1, the overall sense effect on the target position, with shorter RTs for the literal predicates (see Table 4), is significant in the subject analysis, $F_s(1, 59) = 4.34, p < .05$, and marginal in the item analysis, $F_i(1, 11) = 3.94, p < .08$. The pairwise analyses are nonsignificant (all $ps > .1$), except for the comparison between literal–peripheral versus apt metaphors, $F_s(1, 59) = 3.47, p < .07$.

On target2, the overall sense effect is marginal for the subject analysis, $F_s(1, 59) = 3.60, p = .06$, but not significant for the item analysis, $F_i(1, 11) = 3.53, p = .09$. Pairwise analyses do not yield significance (all $ps > .1$), except for the comparison

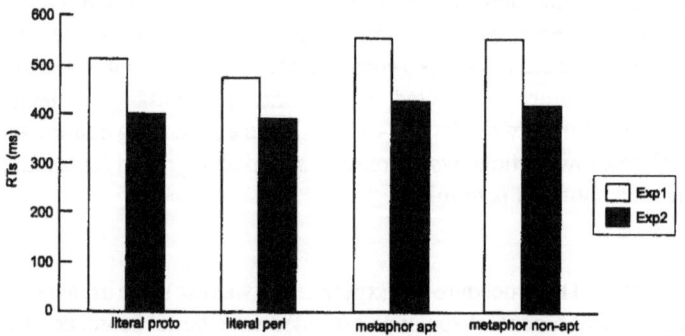

FIGURE 1   Reaction times (RTs) for Experiments 1 and 2, on target.

TABLE 4
Experiment 2: Mean Reaction Times (Msec) and Standard Deviations on Target,
Target2, and Target2 + 1

Condition	Target (= Category Name)		Target2		Target2 + 1	
	M	SD	M	SD	M	SD
Literal, prototype	396	106	449	75	436	151
Literal, peripheral	389	110	503	102	433	109
Metaphor, apt	422	160	525	129	439	151
Metaphor, nonapt	415	152	498	80	480	168

between literal prototypes and apt metaphors, $F_s(1, 59) = 5.36, p < .05; F_i(1, 11) = 5.78, p < .05$.

On target2 + 1, no sense effect can be distinguished between literal and metaphorical conditions, $F_s(1, 59) = 2.99, p < .09; F_i(1, 11) = 1.59, p > .2$. This absence of a sense effect at a rather advanced stage in the processing of the sentence corresponds to what has been found for the same position in Experiment 1. In addition, target2 + 1 in Experiment 2 offers no significant prototype effect within the literal conditions (both $Fs < 1$). Importantly, the effect of aptness was significant at this point, $F_s(1, 59) = 4.93, p < .05; F_i(1, 11) = 4.46, p < .06$. At target2 + 1, apt items were processed as fast as prototypical and peripheral items (no significance, $ps > .10$). In contrast, all comparisons between conditions with nonapt metaphors are significant or marginal; literal–prototypical versus nonapt metaphors: $F_s(1, 59) = 5.47, p < .05; F_i(1, 11) = 4.96, p < .05$; literal–peripheral versus nonapt metaphors: $F_s(1, 59) = 6.35, p < .05; F_i(1, 11) = 5.75, p < .05$. Experiment 2 differs from the first experiment, then, mainly in the emergence of an aptness effect toward the end of a clause, which is even more striking when we consider the item analysis, given the limited number of metaphorical items (12) used in the experiment. Figure 2 summarizes the results for Experiment 2 over the three data points distinguished.

In comparison with Experiment 1, we notice, first of all, the systematically lower RTs for all data points concerned, due to the effect of a preceding context for both literal and metaphorical conditions. Experiment 2 shows an overall sense effect between literal and metaphorical conditions on target and target2. Interestingly, on target2 + 1 the sense effect that disappeared in Experiment 1 is also absent in Experiment 2, but nonapt metaphors perform ostensibly worse at this point (compared to the other conditions for Experiment 2) than in Experiment 1. As noted earlier, it is also at this point that a significant effect could be observed between apt and nonapt metaphors. In fact, we see that it is the metaphorical condition containing apt items that practically coincides with the two literal conditions. In other words, on target2 + 1 apt metaphors behave as if they have been more or less fully interpreted (at least as fully as their literal counterparts), whereas nonapt metaphors continue to cause interpretive difficulties. On the whole, RTs on target2 + 1 for apt metaphors and both types of literal condition are considerably lower than in Experiment 1 (about 75 msec on average).

DISCUSSION

The purpose of our experiments was to provide an online measurement of the processing characteristics involved in the interpretation of unfamiliar metaphors. To this effect, we made a comparison with matched literal sentences, with and without preceding context. In addition, we wanted to find out whether processing speed is determined by degree of prototypicality in literal classifications and degree of aptness in metaphorical ones. RTs were measured within the sentence, instead of calculating global RTs for whole sentences, because possible sense effects might show up in the course of incremental processing and disappear again toward the end, when an inter-

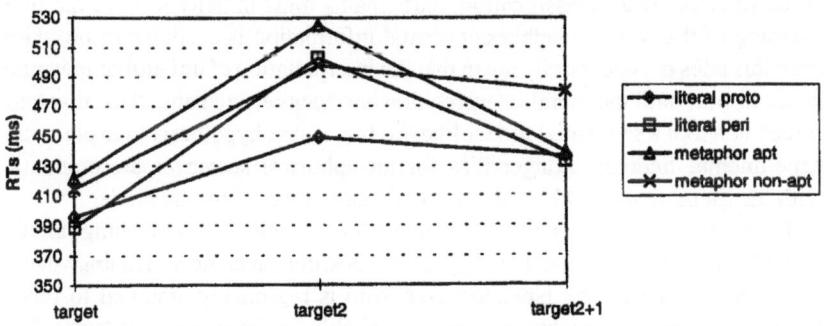

FIGURE 2   Reaction times (RTs) for target, target2, and target2 + 1 (Experiment 2).

pretation has been arrived at. These experiments show that, in the early stages of processing, the comprehension of both apt and nonapt unconventional metaphors is slower than for matched literal sentences. Thus, the results obtained for the early stages of metaphor processing are in line with the types of experimental finding proposed by Gerrig and associates (e.g., Gerrig, 1989; Gerrig & Healy, 1983), who stressed the extra initial processing efforts caused by interpreting familiar words with unfamiliar meanings. However, these findings do not offer any conclusive evidence in favor of or against particular processing models (parallel vs. serial). Toward the end of a sentence (target2 + 1), the distinction in RTs between literal sentences and apt metaphors disappears, although nonapt metaphors continue to perform relatively worse when preceded by context. It is also suggested that, at target2 + 1, apt metaphors preceded by a relevant context are as fully interpreted as their literal counterparts. At this late point in the processing of a sentence, target2 + 1 itself does not instantiate or add to the difference between a literal and a metaphorical interpretation, so that we must attribute the disappearance (apt) or persistence (nonapt) of a sense effect to mechanisms of incremental processing that are at work in the build-up toward this point. The results reported here disconfirm the theoretical preferences advanced by Gibbs (e.g., 1994), who insisted that extra processing resources are not obligatorily devoted to understanding metaphors, conventional or new.

The data on the processing of literal and unfamiliar metaphorical sentences are compatible with a literal first model, in the sense that the initial activation of literal meaning in the course of processing is empirically demonstrated. On target position (i.e., the word at which the literal or metaphorical nature of the sentence becomes clear, always the predicate term), we found a significant sense effect. Metaphorical predicates took longer to read than literal ones. This effect is to be expected when participants have no preceding context sentence which they can use to interpret the metaphor (Experiment 1), but it remained present when a preceding sentence provided them with the ground of the following metaphorical statement (Experiment 2). In other words, on encountering a noun that calls for an unconventional (metaphorical) classification, participants must initially process the literal meaning of this word, whether contextual information is available or not. However, this does not necessarily mean that the interpretation of unfamiliar metaphors needs to wait until the literal interpretation has been rejected and, thus, that one is forced to adopt a sequential model like the literal first hypothesis to explain these experimental findings. Longer RTs for metaphorical sentences are compatible with the literal first model but do not by themselves confirm the model.

Because we are dealing with novel metaphors, in which new meanings are triggered for old words that occupy a predicate position, such new meanings need to be created online by the language user, who is reasonably assumed to rely on meaning representations that are already available for these predicate terms. Thus, the work of sense creation, typical of the interpretation process for unfamiliar metaphors, must operate to supplement ordinary sense selection (i.e., the mere retrieval of existing representations). To fully back a stage model of metaphor comprehension, such as the literal first model, it should be established whether the process of sense creation can only be initiated after sense selection fails (in that the latter process produces an erroneous interpretation). However, the only conclusion that is readily available from these data is that the literal meanings of metaphorically used predicates are indeed activated in the very early stages of processing, not that these literal meanings determine the full extent of the time course involved in the interpretation of this type of metaphor. In particular, a parallel processing model might be equally compatible with the results of both experiments (see Gerrig, 1989). In this scenario, sense selection (or retrieval, for literal meanings) and creation (for figurative ones) operate simultaneously, at least after the processor has established that a new meaning needs to be created in the first place. In short, longer RTs for metaphorical sentences do not automatically imply that the reader can only find a contextually appropriate nonliteral interpretation on the basis of the literal meanings that have been retrieved first.

Interestingly, the sense effect detected on the target position persists at target2, the last word of the syntactic phrase to which the predicate term belongs. It was indicated earlier that, on top of the immediate (incremental) processing that goes on in the interpretation of sentences, potential clause boundaries (e.g., our target2) function as loci of interpretation, or points at which participants attempt to integrate the meaning of the encountered clause material. The fact that the sense effect still turns up at this point in the sentence, even when there is contextual support for interpretation, demonstrates that the interpretation of unfamiliar metaphors is a time-consuming process that lasts well beyond the moment at which the metaphorical term itself is introduced.

One might want to reject this account and attribute the persistent sense effect to an absence of interpretation for the metaphorical conditions in the experiments. According to this line of reasoning, participants experienced the unfamiliar metaphors as instances of noninterpretable language use and did not start, or rapidly aborted, an interpretive routine. However, one particularly salient piece of evidence from Experiment 2 refutes such an interpretation. On target2 + 1, we found that, for the first time in the experimental series, the two groups of metaphors (apt and nonapt) behaved differently. At this position, immediately following the syntactic boundary marked by target2, RTs for apt metaphors were nondistinct from those for literal sentences (the three conditions not differing among each other), whereas RTs for the nonapt metaphors were significantly longer than those for the apt ones. We take this finding to indicate the operation of an interpretation process that is more successful for the apt metaphors than for the nonapt ones. This interpretation process has been initiated on target position and is more time-consuming for all metaphors (hence the sense effect there). It continues up to the final position in the clause, where both types of metaphor still take more processing time than both types of literal sentences (hence the sense effect on target2). On target2 + 1, the divergence between the apt and nonapt metaphors indicates that processing up to target2 has resulted in an acceptable interpretation for the apt metaphors (or that their interpretation has at least been as successful as that for the literal sentences), whereas such an interpretation has not been arrived at for the nonapt metaphors. In Experiment 1, we did not observe the same divergence between the two types of metaphor. Because in this experiment there was no preceding context, the initiated interpretive process on the target position, which was still going on at target2 (hence the sense effect at both positions again), is not likely to be successful for both types of metaphor. Participants may fail to come up with a metaphorical interpretation for lack of sufficient contextual support. If the interpretation runs aground on all metaphorical sentence types, it could be argued that participants may not attempt any further processing and abort the interpretive process to continue with the rest of the sentence. The end of a syntactic clause is a good point for abandoning unsuccessful processing attempts and resetting the semantic processor. This would account for the finding in Experiment 1 that, on target2 + 1, RTs for both metaphor types are statistically nondistinct from those for the literal sentences.

In both experiments, we failed to find a reliable prototype effect within the group of literal sentences; that is, sentences with prototypical subjects were not processed faster than sentences with peripheral ones. This finding was constant across experiments and measurement positions (target, target2, target2 + 1). This is a remarkable finding considering the robustness of prototype effects in a variety of experimental tasks as reported in the literature. Recall that the lack of this effect cannot be due to item selection, as the same subjects and predicates taken from these experiments gave rise to a significant effect in a traditional category verification task (see Experiment 1, Pretest 4). Although further research is required to replicate this effect, we suggest that the category information that is mobilized in the context of a simple reading task differs from the information that comes to bear on the essentially metalinguistic tasks in which prototype effects have been demonstrated (category verification, rating tasks, member generation, etc.). In other words, the lack of a prototype effect in our self-paced reading experiments does not discredit the frequently attested prototype effects but suggests, rather, that the information on which these effects are based is less involved in online sentence processing. Eye-tracking data remain inconclusive in this respect (see Duffy & Rayner, 1990; Liversedge & Underwood, 1998).

Finally, the results reported here are also of some methodological importance. We pointed out earlier that previous research had generally failed to measure processing while participants are reading metaphorical (or, in general, figurative) sentences in real time, relying instead on rather crude measures like total sentence RT (but see Frisson & Pickering, 1999). Our finding of different response patterns at different sentence positions indicates that it is unwise to collapse data across sentence positions in this kind of research (which is the case when total sentence RTs are used). One may well lose important effects, which can turn up at only one theoretically relevant position, if these are drowned in the measurements for whole sentences only. Especially if one wants to make statements on the literal first model, it is risky to neglect the precise time course of processing from the metaphorical term onward. This risk may be particularly high in the domain of familiar metaphors, where an initial processing delay on the metaphorical target itself may rapidly disappear if participants quickly manage to arrive at a metaphorical interpretation (which is not unlikely, given the interpretive success of apt unfamiliar metaphors toward the end of the clause in the present experiments). We emphasize that research on metaphor processing will benefit from the use of experimental techniques that can track the time course of such processing word by word.

ACKNOWLEDGMENTS

Steven Frisson is also affiliated with the University of Glasgow, Department of Psychology, Human Communication Research Centre.

This article is a revised and substantially elaborated version of an earlier preprint: Brisard, Frisson, and Sandra (1999). This study is supported by Grant G.0246.97 from the *Fonds voor Wetenschappelijk Onderzoek – Vlaanderen*.

We thank Kate Nation for helping us out with some of the analyses and allowing us to conduct a small supportive experiment at the University of York.

REFERENCES

Abrams, K., & Bever, T. G. (1969). Syntactic structure modifies attention during speech perception and recognition. *Quarterly Journal of Experimental Psychology, 21*, 280–290.

Blasko, D. G., & Connine, C. M. (1993). Effects of familiarity and aptness on metaphor processing. *Journal of Experimental Psychology: Learning, Memory, and Cognition, 19*, 295–308.

Brisard, F., Frisson, S., & Sandra, D. (1999). Processing unfamiliar metaphors during self-paced reading. In The Japanese Cognitive Science Society (Eds.), *Proceedings of the Second International Conference on Cognitive Science* (pp. 86–91). Tokyo: The Japanese Cognitive Science Society.

Dascal, M. (1989). On the roles of context and literal meaning in understanding. *Cognitive Science, 13*, 253–257.

Duffy, S. A., & Rayner, K. (1990). Eye movements and anaphor resolution: Effects of antecedent typicality and distance. *Language and Speech, 33*, 103–119.

Frazier, L. (1999). *On sentence interpretation.* Dordrecht, The Netherlands: Kluwer.

Frisson, S., & Pickering, M. J. (1999). The processing of metonymy: Evidence from eye movements. *Journal of Experimental Psychology: Learning, Memory, and Cognition, 25*, 1366–1383.

Gerrig, R. J. (1989). The time course of sense creation. *Memory & Cognition, 17*, 194–207.

Gerrig, R. J., & Healy, A. F. (1983). Dual processes in metaphor understanding: Comprehension and appreciation. *Journal of Experimental Psychology: Learning, Memory, and Cognition, 9*, 667–675.

Gibbs, R. W. (1984). Literal meaning and psychological theory. *Cognitive Science, 8*, 275–304.

Gibbs, R. W. (1992). When is metaphor? The idea of understanding in theories of metaphor. *Poetics Today, 13*, 575–606.

Gibbs, R. W. (1994). *The poetics of mind: Figurative thought, language, and understanding.* New York: Cambridge University Press.

Gildea, P., & Glucksberg, S. (1983). On understanding metaphor: The role of context. *Journal of Verbal Learning and Verbal Behavior, 22*, 577–590.

Giora, R. (1997). Understanding figurative and literal language: The graded salience hypothesis. *Cognitive Linguistics, 8,* 183–206.

Glucksberg, S., Gildea, P., & Bookin, H. B. (1982). On understanding nonliteral speech: Can people ignore metaphors? *Journal of Verbal Learning and Verbal Behavior, 21,* 85–98.

Grice, H. P. (1975). Logic and conversation. In P. Cole & J. Morgan (Eds.), *Syntax and semantics* (Vol. 3, pp. 41–58). New York: Academic.

Inhoff, A. W., Lima, S. D., & Carroll, P. J. (1984). Contextual effects on metaphor comprehension in reading. *Memory & Cognition, 12,* 558–567.

Liversedge, S. P., & Underwood, G. (1998). Foveal processing load and landing effects in reading. In G. Underwood (Ed.), *Eye guidance in reading and scene perception* (pp. 201–222). Oxford, England: Elsevier.

McCloskey, M., & Glucksberg, S. (1979). Decision processes in verifying category membership statements: Implications for models of semantic memory. *Cognitive Psychology, 11,* 1–37.

Ortony, A., Schallert, D. L., Reynolds, R. E., & Antos, S. J. (1978). Interpreting metaphors and idioms: Some effects of context on comprehension. *Journal of Verbal Learning and Verbal Behavior, 17,* 465–477.

Searle, J. (1979). Metaphor. In A. Ortony (Ed.), *Metaphor and thought* (pp. 92–123). Cambridge, England: Cambridge University Press.

METAPHOR AND SYMBOL, *16*(1&2), 109–121
Copyright © 2001, Lawrence Erlbaum Associates, Inc.

The Costs and Benefits of Metaphor

Ira A. Noveck

Institut des Sciences Cognitives
Lyon, France

Maryse Bianco and Alain Castry

Département des Sciences de l'Education
Université de Grenoble

Many researchers consider metaphor so fundamental to psychological activity that they claim that it does not require extra cognitive effort to process. We do not dispute that metaphors are natural to human cognition, but we argue that a metaphor's relative ease of use should not be confounded with an expectation that it prompts no extra effort. As many studies show (including those presented here), metaphors often come with costs when compared to nonfigurative controls (e.g., longer processing times). However, we also argue that the extra costs associated with an apt metaphor should come with benefits. This analysis, based on relevance theory, does a good job of accounting for some overlooked psycholinguistic findings concerning metaphor processing.

In this article, we address two accounts of metaphor comprehension. One comes from Gibbs (1994), who argued that, in keeping with Lakoff and Johnson's (1980) seminal view, metaphor is not a special rhetorical device but fundamental to human cognition. He theorized that metaphors serve to map one conceptual domain to another in a reflex-like manner that does not require special cognitive effort. The other approach, based on relevance theory (Sperber & Wilson, 1986/1995), actually shares much with Gibbs's account. Relevance theory also does not consider metaphor to be a special device, viewing it as natural to human cognition. Furthermore, like Gibbs's account, relevance theory resists a classical Gricean or Searlean analysis that assumes that a listener first needs to reject a literal interpretation of a meta-

Requests for reprints should be sent to Ira A. Noveck, Institut des Sciences Cognitives, Centre National de la Recherche Scientifique, 67 Boulevard Pinel, 69675 Bron, France. E-mail: noveck@isc.cnrs.fr

phor to appreciate the metaphor's meaning. Relevance theory differs in that cognitive effort is central to its analysis of utterances in general. Based on a relevance theory analysis, we argue that it is reasonable to expect metaphors to require more effort to process than a nonfigurative equivalent.

In what follows, we briefly describe relevance theory and a cost–benefit explanation of metaphors that the theory inspires. We then review data drawn from a paradigm developed by Gibbs (1990) that indicate that costs are indeed evident in metaphor processing. Albeit to a lesser degree, his data also reveal some benefits for metaphoric processing. Before concluding, we present two developmental studies that buttress our claims based on Gibbs's paradigm. Our ultimate aim is to show how relevance theory can do a good job of accounting for psycholinguistic findings on metaphor.

METAPHORS AS EFFORT-IMPOSING LOOSE TALK

Relevance theory views inference making as a constant feature of communication geared toward gathering in (and sharing) one's intentions. Essential to relevance theory is the claim that, in processing any utterance, people endeavor to draw out as many cognitive effects (i.e., benefits) as possible for the least effort (i.e., cost). Two features of relevance theory are crucial for describing metaphors (see Sperber & Wilson, 1986/1991): (a) Utterances need not be literally true for a listener to draw implications effectively (which is why metaphors are considered a form of loose talk), and (b) a metaphoric utterance is likely to carry more information than a more literal, more direct equivalent. To illustrate, consider a scenario in which a swimming instructor says to a 5-year-old, *You are a tadpole.* The utterance is not literally true while effectively conveying information from teacher to student and it goes further than its literal equivalent (which one can presume is something like *You are a young child doing a frog kick*; at the very least, the instructor's expression is arguably endearing, whereas the literal equivalent is not.

It is this second feature that concerns us here because it is related to the listener's *comprehension* of utterances. Relevance theory essentially argues that the metaphor prompts multitasking. In the *You are a tadpole* example, the metaphor is making reference to the swimming student, plus it is describing something about him and transmitting affection. A neutral expression like *You are a child* in the same context would be doing the reference portion only (and would not seem terribly informative). This comparative analysis leads us to hypothesize that there are (at minimum) two components to a full appreciation of metaphor: understanding what the metaphor is referring to and understanding the interlocutor's intention in using it. Being that it is difficult to imagine that the extra cognitive effects associated with metaphor come cost free, we are led to make two claims. Our primary claim is that it should not be surprising to find evidence supporting the notion that, all other things being equal, metaphors are costly when compared to literal controls. Our auxiliary claim is that the extra costs that come with an apt metaphor should be commensurate with extra benefits. That is, one should be able to find evidence indicating that appreciated metaphors have benefits when compared to nonfigurative equivalents.

The preceding analysis brings together three strands of metaphor research that might, at first glance, appear unrelated. One concerns studies showing that compared to literal controls, there are costs associated with metaphors either in terms of comprehension among children (Vosniadou, Ortony, Reynolds, & Wilson, 1984) or in terms of longer reading times among adults (e.g., Gerrig & Healy, 1983). A second comes from Williams-Whitney, Mio, and Whitney (1992), who established a link between available effort and metaphor production. They showed that 3rd- and 4th-year college students are more likely than a select group of 1st-year students to produce novel metaphors in writing about an imaginary character or about themselves. That is, as more resources become available with age or perhaps skill, novel metaphors are more likely to crop up. The third strand is based on work indicating that metaphors have implicit benefits that can lead to deeper encoding of materials. Reynolds and Schwartz (1983) showed how a paragraph having a metaphoric conclusion, as opposed to a literal one, consistently leads to higher (immediate and delayed) "memorability" of both the conclusion and its context. These three strands of research taken together indicate that metaphors are costly, but they have the potential to provide benefits. Our experiments attempt to demonstrate this while employing one overarching procedure.

GIBBS'S METAPHORIC REFERENCE PARADIGM

We turn to Gibbs's account of metaphor processing and begin by noting his skepticism about relevance theory's approach. In his book, Gibbs (1994) wrote:

> [The] psychological research ... clearly shows that listeners do not ordinarily devote extra processing resources to understanding metaphors compared with more literal utterances. The metaphor-as-loose-talk view ... incorrectly assumes that metaphors, and other tropes such as irony, obligatorily demand additional cognitive effort to be understood. (p. 232)

Part of Gibbs's claim about the ordinary nature of metaphor processing comes from his own paradigms. Consider the findings from the following experiment in which metaphors are shown to be as efficient as nonmetaphors in making reference to a previously mentioned item in a text (Gibbs, 1990). Gibbs presented participants with eight lines of a story before presenting one of three different concluding sentences that vary with respect to their referential content. For example, the following story (1a–h) concerns a weak boxer and a boxing match and lines 2 through 4 were one of its concluding sentences:

1. (a) Stu went to see the Saturday night fights.
    (b) There was one boxer that Stu hated.
    (c) This guy always lost.
    (d) Just as the match was supposed to start, Stu went to get some snacks.
    (e) He stood in line ten minutes.
    (f) When he returned, the bout had been canceled.
    (g) "What happened?" Stu asked a friend.
    (h) The friend replied,
2. The creampuff didn't even show up.
3. The fighter didn't even show up.
4. The referee didn't even show up.

Sentences 2 and 3 are, respectively, metaphoric and synonymous references to the same character, the hated boxer. Sentence 4, which makes reference to a previously unmentioned referee, served as a control. Gibbs found that the average reading time for control sentences like Sentence 4 was not significantly different from the reading times for Sentences 2 or 3. Thus, Gibbs was not convinced that metaphors required relatively more effort to process. He also gave prominence to a probe task, in which the participant was required to determine quickly whether a particular word appeared previously in the story. A relatively quick "yes" response to the earlier instantiated referent of the metaphoric term could be a measure of processing benefit. For example, a "yes" response to the word *boxer* after reading Sentence 2 would signal that the metaphor served to prime the referent. Although Gibbs found a facilitation for probes following metaphoric conclusions (1,118 msec) compared to the control condition's conclusions (1,331 msec), he also found that the synonymous condition's probes led to latencies (1,229 msec) that were statistically comparable to the metaphoric condition's probes. Thus, he took the metaphoric references to be as efficient as synonymous ones.

The results from this experiment actually underline how the comprehension of metaphors appears to require some effort and to provide some benefits. We point to two of his main findings. First, the mean reading time of Gibbs's (1990) control sentences is actually intermediate (1,867 msec) between metaphoric sentences like Sentence 2 (2,117 msec) and synonymous sentences like Sentence 3 (1,735 msec); the analysis as reported did not capture the distinction of interest, which is that a sentence containing a metaphoric reference took significantly longer to read than its synonymous counterpart. Comparisons to the control sentence, which in the case of Sentence 4 leads to different kinds of implications than those conveyed by referring to the boxer, are far less revealing than the metaphor–synonym distinction. Second, reactions to the probes in the metaphor condition tended to be faster (and less error prone) than those in the synonymous formulation condition. Gibbs's findings suggest that there are processing costs associated with metaphoric references, but that these terms have the potential to provide benefits as well.

THE EXPERIMENTS

To investigate our account of metaphor comprehension, we have adopted Gibbs's (1990) reference paradigm described earlier. We began with two goals. One was to verify that unanticipated metaphoric formulations do indeed require extra effort when compared to synonymous ones as measured through reading times (i.e., confirm the finding that Gibbs tended to disregard).[1] The other was to determine whether we can find evidence showing that a by-product of extra effort is added benefits. To test our hypotheses, we investigated development. Aside from the fact that minimal competence with metaphors among children would add support to claims favoring the naturalness and ubiquity of metaphor, we anticipated that evidence of effort should be even clearer among developing readers.

We now make two concrete predictions based on the supposition that there are at least two components to a full appreciation of metaphor: (a) detecting the referent of the metaphor and (b) comprehending an added effect (e.g., something that tells the reader more about the author's or character's intention). All readers are compelled to do extra processing when faced with an informationally rich metaphoric reference instead of a synonymous one. Thus, there should be evidence showing that all readers require more time to understand a metaphoric reference than a synonymous control. For our second prediction, assume that both a child and an adult have a fixed amount of time (say .5 sec) to integrate a read line of text with previous information. In that fixed amount of time, an adult should be able to integrate more information (references, intentions, attitudes, etc.) than a younger reader. Compared to a synonymous reference, the appearance of the metaphor (the imposed extra effort) risks undermining an immature reader's comprehension with respect to (a), (b), or both. In contrast, the appearance of the metaphor for a competent reader should lead to the attainment of both (a) and (b), leading to a richer appreciation of the text through the metaphoric reference when compared to the synonymous equivalent. This analysis should be reflected by rates of correct responses to follow-up questions. Because of space limitations, we summarize briefly the findings from two experiments.

---

[1] If too many cues anticipate the metaphor, the metaphor would be effectively primed and its informational impact would be reduced. For example, the metaphoric appeal of (and difficulty in comprehending) *You are a piglet* would be diminished if the referent was anticipated in a context stuffed with farms, pens, mud, youngsters, oinking, and so on. Our paradigm tried to avoid such scenarios.

General Method

The stories in our experiments were in French and were modeled on Gibbs's (1990) paradigm described earlier with one modification: We avoided placing the metaphoric or synonymous references in the concluding line. Sixteen eight-line texts were prepared that had, as the penultimate line, a sentence containing either a metaphoric or synonymous reference to a previously mentioned item. For example, consider the (translated) story in Example 5 and the metaphor in the second to last line (5g):

5. (a) The second-grade pupils went to the pool with their teacher.
    (b) The lifeguard organized a few games for them.
    (c) He then asked that they do a few laps.
    (d) Before the end of the class, the phone rang.
    (e) The lifeguard went to answer it.
    (f) Returning, he cried out:
    (g) "All toads to the side of the pool."
    (h) The class went to the lockers and back to school.

In the synonymous formulation condition, the second to last line (5g') read as:

(g') "All students to the side of the pool."

Both toads (*crapauds* in French) and students (*étudiants*) refer to the pupils (*élèves*). In view of the example from Gibbs's paper, we included conventionalized metaphors among our stories, but we tried to avoid them (*crapauds* is an example of a conventionalized metaphor in French).

Experiment 1.   Two hundred and thirty children between the ages of 8 and 12 were presented the 16 stories on paper. Table 1 includes a list of the 16 referred terms, metaphors, and synonyms used. The stories were divided up into in two sets, A and B. Those who received the metaphoric versions of the stories in Set A received the synonymous versions of the stories in Set B, and vice versa. Four random orders were prepared. All the stories provided questions that directly asked about the referent, and all the questions required a "yes" or "no" response. For example, with respect to Example 5, the question (presented while the text was available) was *Were the pupils the ones who went to the side of the pool?* Regardless of formulation (metaphoric or synonymous), the correct response is "yes."

Table 2 presents a summary of the results from the first experiment. A 5 (age: 8, 9, 10, 11, 12) × 2 (reference type: synonymous vs. metaphoric reference) analysis of variance (ANOVA) with repeated measures on the second factor was conducted. We found two revealing effects and no interaction. First, there was a main effect for

TABLE 1
List of Initial Referents and Their Respective Metaphoric and Synonymous
References as Used in Experiment 1

No.	Initial Term	Metaphoric Reference	Synonymous Reference
1.	animateur	perroquet	présentateur
2.	élèves	crapauds	enfants
3.	aspirateur	tank	machine
4.	écharpe	serpent	cache-nez
5.	Jean-Pierre	gorille	maître-nageur
6.	chat	fauve	félin
7.	héron	requin	oiseau
8.	projecteur	bécane	appareil
9.	automobile	baignoire	voiture
10.	Marie et ses copains	étourneaux	petits
11.	La mère du Président	pie	dame
12.	avion	rapace	appareil
13.	autruche	tornade	oiseau
14.	éléphante	bombe	bête
15.	citrouille	monstre	potiron
16.	flute	rossignol	instrument

Note. Metaphoric references for 2, 8, and 11 are conventional, and those in 5 and 15 can be construed as such in appropriate contexts.

TABLE 2
Percentage of Correct Responses to Reference Questions Among Children Between
8 and 12 Years of Age

	Age				
Reference	8[a]	9[b]	10[c]	11[a]	12[b]
Metaphoric	79	85	88	87	92
Synonymous	87	90	95	94	95

Note. An example of a reference question is "Were the pupils (*élèves*) the ones who went to the side of the pool?," where the metaphoric reference was toads (*crapauds*) and the synonymous reference was students (*étudiants*).
[a]$n = 41$. [b]$n = 51$. [c]$n = 46$.

age, $F(4, 75) = 2.771$, $p < .05$. This shows that referential ability in general improves with age. Second, formulations containing synonymous references consistently prompted higher rates of correct responses than those containing metaphoric ones, $F(1, 75) = 22.852$, $p < .0005$. In fact, formulations with synonymous references provide rates of correct responses that are consistently about 7% higher than those with metaphoric ones until around 12 years of age. Among 12-year-olds, one sees the gap between metaphoric and synonymous reference comprehension closing: The 12-year-olds showed that formulations with synonymous references led to rates of correct performance that were only 2.6% superior to those prompted by formulations having metaphoric references (94.9% vs. 92.3%). This indicates that metaphors do come with a small risk of leading young readers astray, but the risk appears to diminish progressively with age.

All responses are clearly above chance levels, so one can conclude that children are quite competent at detecting and accounting for a metaphoric reference; however, these results indicate that unexpected metaphors do impose a burden on the reader. This would account for the slight, consistent advantage (in terms of rates of correct responses) associated with stories containing the synonymous formulations among younger readers. Note that this effect is evident despite the fact that children have full access to their texts.

Experiment 2. To further substantiate our claim that metaphoric references indeed impose a burden and thus take additional effort to process, we introduced an online version of this task. There were 50 nine-year-olds, 48 eleven-year-olds, 51 fourteen-year-olds, and 40 adults. The 9-, 11-, and 14-year-olds were presented 12 of the 16 stories from Experiment 1. Adults were presented all 16 stories from Experiment 1 plus filler items (concerning deductive inference). Thus, the adult data came from a more demanding session. All analyses concern only those stories that were seen by both the children and adults.

As in Experiment 1, the stories were divided up into in two sets, A and B. Those who received the metaphoric versions of the stories in Set A received the synonymous versions of the stories in Set B, and vice versa. The number of participants who received Set A was roughly equal in size to the number who received Set B for all age groups. As in Gibbs's (1990) original paradigm, the stories were presented randomly, by computer, one line at a time. Reading was self-paced, and the participants' reading times for the metaphoric and synonymous formulations were measured. The materials were reworked only slightly to verify that sentence length of the critical line (like 5g's) was roughly equivalent across stories (between 9 and 13 syllables). Each story was accompanied by one of three kinds of follow-up questions requiring a "yes" or "no" response: (a) a question about a detail of the story, (b) a general comprehension question, or (c) a question like the one in Experiment 1 concerning the referent. Only one kind of question was presented after each story, but, for example, these three kinds of questions about the story in Example 5 would be: (a) Were the students in the second grade? (detail); (b) Was the lifeguard interrupted during the class? (general comprehension); and (c) Were the pupils the ones to go to the side of the pool? (referent). Unlike in this example, correct responses often required "no" responses. Note that this reading task is more difficult than the one in the first experiment (especially for younger readers) in that memory load is more critical here.

We analyze the results concerning the reading time of the crucial penultimate line as well as correct responses to the questions posed. We point out that one story was removed from all analyses because a programming error presented the story (line 9 in Table 1) in its metaphoric guise throughout to the children. We also note that we did not filter out reading times; that is, all reading times from the 11 remaining stories were included in the analysis. Two other stories (stories for referents 14 and 15) were removed from the analyses concerning rates of correct responses only because the questions were not clear and led to responses that were difficult to interpret (e.g., one question was *Grenouillette doesn't have much imagination?* when the story indicated that she did; either one of the response options—"yes" or "no"—does not capture a correct response). A summary of the results is presented in Table 3.

We turn first to the reading time results. A 4 (age: 9, 11, 14, adults) × 2 (reference type: synonymous vs. metaphoric reference) ANOVA with repeated measures on the second factor was conducted. The results revealed a main effect for age, $F(3, 40) = 53.6, p = .0001$; a main effect for reference type, $F(1, 40) = 44.8, p = .0001$; and an Age × Reference Type interaction, $F(3, 40) = 7.6, p < .0005$. It is not surprising that reading speed increases with age. More interesting is that, at each age, one finds that sentences containing the metaphoric reference are read more slowly than those containing the synonymous control and that the gap closes with age, although never completely. The adult data, confirming Gibbs's (1990), shows that metaphoric references prompt a slowdown when compared to synonymous controls.

To analyze rates of correct responses, a 4 (age: 9, 11, 14, adults) × 2 (reference type: synonymous vs. metaphoric reference) ANOVA with repeated measures on the

TABLE 3
Children's and Adults' Mean Speed of Reading the Line Containing Either a Metaphoric or Synonymous Reference (Plus the Mean Rates of Correct Responses to Stories' Subsequent Question)

Age	n	Reference Type	
		Metaphoric	*Synonymous*
9-year-olds	50	7,908 msec (74%)	5,586 msec (82%)
11-year-olds	48	4,510 msec (73%)	3,842 msec (77%)
14-year-olds	51	3,609 msec (86%)	2,967 msec (87%)
Adults	40	2,851 msec (90%)	2,321 msec (83%)

Note. Reading times are based on 11 texts and rates of correct responses are based on 9 of these. Unlike the children, the adults viewed filler items.

second factor was conducted. The only effect that even approached significance was the Age × Reference Type interaction, $F(3, 32) = 2.76, p = .058$. The interaction is an indication of evolving benefits with age. The rates of correct responses show that the youngest children, like in Experiment 1, pay a small price in comprehension when they encounter a metaphoric reference. Adults reveal that the metaphoric reference actually aids comprehension slightly. We remain cautious about our second finding because, as indicated earlier, the adult data were collected from an experiment that also included filler stories. Nevertheless, the pattern of results is consistent with the cost–benefit analysis that led to our initial predictions.

To summarize, Experiment 1 showed that for the developing reader it is easier to make links with a previously mentioned term (to the referent) when the reference is synonymous with the term rather than metaphoric. Experiment 1 also indicated that this advantage decreases with age. Experiment 2 revealed the extent of this developmental effect. It showed that for the youngest children the rate of correct responses to follow-up questions was lower when a metaphoric reference had been used, as in Experiment 1; for the adults, the rate of correct responses to follow-up questions was higher when a metaphoric reference had been used. The youngest children seem to suffer somewhat when faced with the metaphor and adults seem to benefit. Experiment 2 also showed that, compared to synonymous controls, metaphoric references are consistently associated with relatively longer reading times.

CONCLUSIONS

By drawing on relevance theory, we anticipated that the comprehension of a metaphoric reference is more demanding than that of a synonymous one; that is, there is an extra cost in processing a well-chosen metaphor. Universally longer reading times for sentences containing unanticipated metaphoric references is one piece of evidence revealing of costs. A second is younger readers' lower rates of correct responses when questions followed a metaphoric reference instead of a synonymous one. However, the metaphoric reference has the potential to yield benefits. The slightly higher rates of correct responses among adults when questions followed a metaphoric reference instead of a synonymous one is an indication that metaphors offer multiple effects.

We consider our data pointing to costs clear. Evidence in favor of benefits is less abundant. This is partly due to the fact that our follow-up questions did not necessarily tap into unique aspects of each metaphoric reference. For instance, an added effect of the *toads* reference in line 5g might well be something related to affection, whereas the added effect of another metaphor (consider *tank* as a reference for *vacuum cleaner*) might be descriptive (i.e., it is loud and clunky). In both cases, the story's follow-up question did not touch on the invited features of the respective metaphors. We predict clearer support for our claims about benefits when the metaphor's implicit effects can be specified for each individual case. If one does not find stronger supporting evidence for benefits when the follow-up questions are better controlled, it would present a challenge for our account. Generally speaking, to undermine our analysis one would have to show that an unanticipated, apt, and appreciated metaphor violates our cost–benefit analysis. This demonstrates how our application of relevance theory is testable.

How would relevance theory account for those cases that indicate less effort (e.g., faster reading times relative to nonfigurative controls) for sentences or words that had been used metaphorically? We respond by taking a careful look at a set of studies by Allbritton, McKoon, and Gerrig (1995), who showed that a sentence like *"Both sides were now bringing out their heavy artillery"* was read significantly faster (as a target in a priming task after it had been read once in a story) when it had been a metaphoric conclusion rather than a plausible literal conclusion. We make two points. First, when a metaphoric formulation is shown to be advantageous compared to a literal one (in terms of faster reading times), it is arguably due to important changes in their respective contexts. For example, in Allbritton et al.'s Experiment 1, the context that rendered metaphoric *"Both sides were now bringing out their heavy artillery"* provided an elaborate description of two friends' debating tendencies, making this sentence readily understood. As the authors noted, the control condition was potentially less clear; comprehension of this critical line could have suffered from an earlier change in topic. The upshot is that the context for the primed sentence was sufficiently rich for accessing the metaphor in the metaphoric condition and arguably obscure in the control condition.[2] Second, their priming study allows one to tap into encoding. Thus, much like in Reynolds and Schwartz (1983), the Allbritton et al. work can be taken to show that the clearly signaled metaphor provided some benefits to the participant when it was first read and that these carried over to the priming study. Gibbs's (1990) probe results can be similarly construed.

That metaphoric comprehension can be easily affected by context is well known. Cues need only be minimal to reduce the effort involved in comprehending metaphors (see Pynte, Besson, Robichon, & Poli, 1996, who showed this nicely with the aid of evoked potentials). Any claims about effort are relative to a provided context. The work reported here shows that metaphors can be seen to be costly in contexts that are arguably neutral otherwise.

---

[2]To address this issue of obscurity, their final experiment provided only the richly described metaphoric condition and presented either the metaphoric conclusion or a neutral nonfigurative conclusion. They found that a key term in their metaphoric condition served as a better prime (e.g., *artillery*) for a target word (e.g., *battling*) than did a key term from a neutral control (e.g., *points*). However, the metaphoric term was arguably endowed with richer meaning than the neutral term because the entire paragraph referred to the notions critical to the metaphor (*debates* and *combat,* etc.). Thus, the comprehension of the metaphoric term came with more benefits than the neutral one in the first phase of the experiment. This was arguably demonstrated when the metaphor was later used as a prime.

To sum up, we have pointed out that Gibbs, among others, gave the strong impression that metaphors are not costly. We were skeptical of this claim, especially if the implication is that literal expressions are serviceable replacements for their metaphoric counterparts. We have investigated metaphoric references to detail our argument. We have shown that results from Gibbs's studies support our contention that metaphors come with some processing cost. Inspired by an alternative approach, relevance theory, we have argued that metaphors can be analyzed in terms of costs and benefits. Our findings show that (a) compared to controls, metaphoric references consistently prompt longer reading times; and (b) in terms of comprehension, metaphoric references are sources of difficulty for younger children and sources of potential benefit for adults. We thus hope we have shown that a metaphoric reference is an imposition on a reader, but its potential for impact is linked with an ability to appreciate its intended meaning.

ACKNOWLEDGMENTS

We very much appreciated the comments and the discussion that followed from the presentation of this work at the Artificial Intelligence and the Simulation of Behaviour conference in Edinburgh, Scotland (1999). We thank John Barnden, Ingar Brinck, Dick Carter, Craig Hamilton, David Nicolas, Dan Sperber, and two anonymous reviewers for some very helpful comments on an earlier draft.

REFERENCES

Allbritton, D. W., McKoon, G., & Gerrig, R. J. (1995). Metaphor-based schemas and text representations: Making connections through conceptual metaphors. *Journal of Experimental Psychology: Learning, Memory and Cognition, 21,* 612–625.

Gerrig, R. J., & Healy, A. F. (1983). Dual processes in metaphor understanding: Comprehension and appreciation. *Journal of Experimental Psychology: Learning, Memory and Cognition, 9,* 667–675.

Gibbs, R. (1990). Comprehending figurative referential descriptions. *Journal of Experimental Psychology: Learning, Memory and Cognition, 16,* 56–66.

Gibbs, R. (1994). *The poetics of mind: Figurative thought, language, and understanding.* New York: Cambridge University Press.

Lakoff, G., & Johnson, M. (1980). *Metaphors we live by.* Chicago: University of Chicago Press.

Pynte, J., Besson, M., Robichon, F.-H., & Poli, J. (1996). The time-course of metaphor comprehension: An event-related potential study. *Brain and Language, 55,* 293–316.

Reynolds, R. E., & Schwartz, R. M. (1983). Relation of metaphoric processing to comprehension and memory. *Journal of Educational Psychology, 75,* 450–459.

Sperber, D., & Wilson, D. (1991). Loose talk. In S. Davis (Ed.), *Pragmatics: A reader* (pp. 540–549). New York: Oxford University Press. (Original work published 1986)

Sperber, D., & Wilson, D. (1995). *Relevance: Communication and cognition.* Oxford, England: Blackwell. (Original work published 1986)

Vosniadou, S., Ortony, A., Reynolds, R. E., & Wilson, P. T. (1984). Sources of difficulty in children's comprehension of metaphorical language. *Child Development, 55,* 1588–1607.

Williams-Whitney, D., Mio, J. S., & Whitney, P. (1992). Metaphor production in creative writing. *Journal of Psycholinguistic Research, 21,* 497–509.

METAPHOR AND SYMBOL, *16*(1&2), 123–142

Is Metaphor Universal? Cross-Language Evidence From German and Japanese

Christoph Neumann

Department of Computer Science
Tokyo Institute of Technology

Formal considerations show that monolingual metaphor study is caught in a circularity of evidence in trying to account for the cognitive nature of metaphor. Cross-lingual evidence, however, may circumvent this circularity. In a cross-language study, 106 analogous metaphors in German and Japanese are presented as evidence for the existence of a language-independent mechanism responsible for metaphor production. A definition for similarity as well as a formal classification system for cross-language metaphors is established. Although this study does not account for cognitive metaphor schemas in general, the semantic domains of the metaphors found indicate a universal tendency toward metaphorizing embodied experiences.

In this article, I aim to furnish evidence on the (cognitive) status of metaphors from a cross-language perspective. If two languages display similar metaphors that have arisen independently, this will be a strong indication about the status of the metaphor mechanism itself and of the involved semantic domains. I chose Japanese and German because of their low level of language contact.

THE COGNITIVE CLAIM

Whereas in traditional linguistics, metaphor was a stylistic means that "arbitrarily" affected single words (*Metzler Lexikon Sprache,* 1993, p. 388), most proponents of contemporary metaphor theory consider metaphor to be a cognitive, nonlinguistic process: "Metaphor is the main mechanism through which we comprehend abstract

Requests for reprints should be sent to Christoph Neumann, Department of Computer Science, Tokyo Institute of Technology, 2–12–1, O-okayama, Meguro-ku, Tokyo, 152 Japan. E-mail: neumann@cs.titech.ac.jp

concepts and perform abstract reasoning" (Lakoff, 1993, p. 235). This process (henceforth called *metaphorization*) connects two specific concept clusters (target and source domains; e.g., *love* and *journey*). Although researchers are divided over the nature of this abstract relation between concept clusters—conceptual metaphors (Gibbs, 1996) versus structural similarity relations (Murphy, 1996)—there is agreement that it is via such a cognitive relation that words acquire figurative readings. For instance, an English speaker immediately understands the figurative use of *obstacle* in *"Her mother is a real obstacle to our relationship"* as *"Her mother is a real problem for our relationship"* because journey obstacles are related to love problems via a *"LOVE IS A JOURNEY"* metaphor.

This cognitive claim implies that metaphorical mappings may be universal or language independent, if they involve semantic domains like embodied experiences that are independent of the conceptual system of one language (Gibbs, 1996). Lakoff (1987) called such unmarked domains "preconceptual" (p. 278), as opposed to culturally marked domains. The alleged language independence of metaphorization is probably the reason why, for instance, Caramelli and Venturi (1999) quoted test metaphors presented to Italian test participants not in the original Italian, but only in the English translation, and seemed to implicitly assume that speakers of Italian and English share a universal metaphorical layout.

However, the cognitive claim has been attacked (sometimes from within its own ranks) as not furnishing enough nonlinguistic evidence (Glucksberg & McGlone, 1999; Murphy, 1996, 1997). Murphy (1996) showed that the conceptual status of alleged metaphors relating source and target as suggested by the Lakoffian school (Gibbs, 1996) is tautologically founded ("circularity of evidence," p. 183): On one hand, conceptual metaphors are identified on the basis of idioms and collocations; on the other hand, these idioms and collocations serve as evidence for the existence of conceptual metaphors (Murphy, 1996). However, this circularity also applies to Murphy's alternative proposal to account for metaphorical phenomena by a mere structural similarity between source and target domain: It is still through idioms and collocations that allegedly similarly structured domains are defined, and these idioms and collocations are used as evidence for the structural similarity of their respective domains.

The lack of conclusive evidence for cognitive concept clusters being involved in the metaphor process, however, questions the very cognitive character of the general process of metaphorization: If the cognitive foundation of metaphor cannot be accounted for in detail, it cannot be generalized as a whole.

While heterogeneous results from attempts to supply nonlinguistic (mostly psychological and statistical) evidence (cf. Gibbs, 1996; Glucksberg & McGlone, 1999; Murphy, 1997) have not allowed conclusions to be drawn on the nature of metaphor, I propose a different research direction: the cross-lingual study of similar metaphors. The vast majority of studies on metaphor are monolingual; that is, theories on cognitive or explicitly universal metaphorical relations are illustrated by data from a single language. I show in what follows that the cross-lingual study of metaphor can furnish methodologically sound evidence for the cognitive status of metaphor, as cannot be derived from a monolingual perspective.

CROSS-LINGUAL METAPHOR STUDY

Cross-Lingual Similarity

The fact that, in English, we can use *traveler* to mean *lover, obstacle* to mean *problem,* and *vehicles* to represent *relationships* does not provide strong evidence that there is actually a cognitive mapping (conceptual metaphor or structural similarity) between the domains *journey* and *love* that these concepts respectively belong to. The figurative usage of these words is merely consistent with there being such a mapping (circular evidence).

However, if the German words for traveler, obstacle, and vehicle also map to the German equivalents of lover, problem, and relationship, it would become much more likely that the two bundles of component mapping relations in English and German arise from a common cognitive mapping between domains, rather than that the same bundles arise coincidentally in two languages without any backing in a cognitive mapping.

Before entering into a broad search for such similar expressions in two languages, we have to clarify the notion of similarity. I define similarity here as *dictionary equivalence*; that is, looking up one element's entry in a bilingual dictionary yields the other element.[1] Expression tuples will become the subject of this study, and metaphor is produced if looking up a given expression in the first language (L1) yields an equivalent for at least two separately marked meanings in the second language (L2).[2] For example, the entry of the German verb *brechen* in the Pons dictionary of German and English (*Pons Kompaktwörterbuch Englisch-Deutsch/Deutsch-Englisch,* 1982) is divided into several subentries, the first of which yields the English 'to break' (marked as the general translation). Another subentry refers to the fixed expression *(mit jemandem) brechen* in the meaning of "to end a relationship," translated into English as 'to break (with some one).' These

---

[1]The dictionary look-up method has the advantage that we can avoid having to resort to semantic definitions of meanings of words like "A traveler is a person on a journey," and also, in the figurative sense, a person that loves, because, apart from the obvious difficulty in finding neutral descriptions, such definitions would be biased as they would have to be based in one language for both languages involved. Of course, dictionary look-ups are still not entirely free of semantics, as they involve looking up general semantic information.

[2]The dictionary check is open to criticisms of being biased, as dictionaries tend to yield the same L2 word for several meanings of the L1 word. This bias can be alleviated by focusing on additional semantic notes in good dictionaries, by having a neutral language (L3) mediate the dictionary check (L1–L3 dictionary; L2–L3 dictionary), or by using monolingual encyclopedias.

two separate correlations would make the tuple (*brechen,* 'break') a viable candidate for cross-lingual metaphor study. This straightforward definition of similarity requires only slight modifications to account for idiomatic expressions and compound nouns.

Our reliance on dictionaries forces us to narrow the study to *dead metaphors.* Normally, the metaphorization process involves two stages of word formation: spontaneous or ad hoc metaphors, and dead or lexicalized (conventional) metaphors. Ad hoc metaphors are constructed on the run and are valid within a single text. To allow for a cross-lingual comparison of ad hoc metaphors, however, we would need a bilingual individual making simultaneous utterances about a single event in L1 and L2. On the other hand, dead metaphors were originally ad hoc metaphors, the meaning of which has entered the lexicon of a linguistic community so that now any speaker at any time may use the expression in its metaphorical sense. Their main research advantage over ad hoc metaphors is that they are accessible through dictionaries, a more objective and readily verifiable reference.

These considerations have been theoretical in character. Our interest now is to see if there are actual cross-lingual metaphors that would validate these considerations.

Other Cross-Linguistic Studies of Metaphor

Several researchers have, in fact, carried out cross-lingual studies on metaphor. In a certain sense, all studies within the Lakoffian framework that focus on languages other than English are cross-lingual, as they classify meaning shifts in the examined languages according to mappings originally based on evidence from English.

However, to the extent of my knowledge, no cross-lingual study has been able to furnish systematic or formal evidence for or against the cognitive claim. Most studies seem to be stuck in a cross-lingual version of the circularity of evidence mentioned earlier: Using the Lakoffian framework, they take the cognitive claim for granted and aim merely at furnishing more evidence for it. Thus, Neagu (1999) supported the metaphor *"HUMANS ARE PLANTS"* through evidence from Romanian, and Liu and Su (1999) discussed the application of metaphors for marriage in Chinese, but both failed to question the underlying assumptions of the paradigm they used. These studies are interesting, as they examine metaphorical structures in languages other than English, but they fail methodologically to furnish theoretical evidence for or against the cognitive claim.

Most explicitly cross-lingual studies also do not qualify as candidates for a cross-lingual metaphor study because of the closeness of the languages in focus. English and German, as used earlier to illustrate the framework of our study, would have to be ruled out in a real study: The two languages are etymologically, culturally, and geographically so close that lexical similarities may in most cases be attributed to direct language contact and not to independent cognitive settings of German and English speakers. Faulstich's (1999) approach sets out to provide cognitive evidence for metaphor by contrasting Italian and Portuguese newspaper accounts of the same event (the European monetary union), using two languages that are likely to use similar words and metaphors to present the same material. Her study thus succeeds in the difficult task of simulating simultaneous metaphor production (mentioned earlier as the condition of comparability of ad hoc metaphors). However, Italian and Portuguese have a common ancestor, Latin, that may simply have passed on parallel constructions to the two languages. Also, formal similarity between languages as closely related as these two makes it very easy to transfer meaning shifts by bilingual speakers, due to their belonging to the same cultural paradigm.[3] In the same way, the metaphors in various European languages that Sweetser (1990) presented must be ruled out as cognitive evidence because of the linguistic closeness of these languages.

Finally, Kamei and Wakao (1992) did not adhere to the Lakoffian school and further used distant languages: They discovered universal features in metonym interpretation for Chinese–English machine translation. Unfortunately, their approach cannot be extended to general metaphor analysis, as they used compositional feature structures as the framework for their work. The compositional paradigm per se, however, prevents any semantic evaluation of metaphor as detailed in Lakoff (1987).

An ideal cross-lingual study would present distant languages from a neutral perspective. This is what I carried out, as detailed in the next section.

SIMILAR METAPHORS IN GERMAN AND JAPANESE

In the following, I present a set of similar expressions in Japanese and German using the same metaphor. This corpus will serve as the basis for a collection of truly language-independent metaphors (without prior commitment to their cognitive status). The classification system of the expression tuples is also new; it is based on formal, not semantic criteria, and will establish a taxonomy for future cross-language metaphor research.

Why Japanese and German?

Japanese and German are ideal candidates for a contrastive metaphor study. They are distant languages, not only geographically, but also typologically and etymo-

---

[3]Similar meaning shifts occur also between English and German, two Germanic languages. The term *site* for URLs on the Internet has thus been readily translated into German as the phonetically and graphically similar *Seite* ('page'), reinforced by the use of *page* in the same sense in English (*home page*), although *site* in the general sense is translated as *Ort* ('location').

logically: German is an Indo-European language, whereas Japanese belongs to the Altaic group. Furthermore, contact between the languages was literally forbidden by Japan's self-imposed isolation until 1853. In the years since then, Japanese has borrowed *"loan"* metaphors from German, especially in scientific fields. For example, *hinketsu* ('blood poverty' = 'anemia') is a literal translation of the German *Blutarmut.* Despite this, the entries in our corpus are not scientific terms, but describe objects or abstract concepts that were already present in Japanese and German before their direct contact. All these considerations point to a high probability of any similar metaphors in the corpus having arisen independently. This is supported by the fact that the *Kougojiten* (1989) lists, for some of the metaphorical readings like *amai* ('sweet,' e.g., *"GOOD IS SWEET"*), examples from classical Japanese literature.

German–Japanese Corpus

I decided to search for similar metaphors in Japanese and German. This corpus contains 106 metaphorical expressions that are similar in both languages. I deliberately avoided biasing the search by a preference for certain semantic domains (like collecting all body-related metaphors or looking for the equivalent of the *"LOVE IS A JOURNEY"* metaphor), as I did not set out to prove a certain semantic preference, but to collect the largest number of metaphor tuples possible.[4] Part of the corpus was based on the analysis of nine articles from the online edition of *Der Spiegel,* a German newsmagazine known for its sophisticated, yet colloquial style, and thus rich in metaphors. In the total of 6,612 words, I found 213 expressions instantiating metaphorical use in 220 (3.33%) occurrences. These metaphors were cross-referenced with a Japanese dictionary, yielding the high number of 41 similar metaphors (19.25% of all identified metaphors). Six of these were excluded because language contact could not be excluded as the reason for similarity,[5] so that I was able to collect in total 35 corpus entries from the newsmagazine analysis. The remaining 71 entries in the corpus were unsystematic occurrences picked up in daily life.

The collected expressions are lexematic expressions—that is, words, compound words, or idiomatic expressions. Corpus entries include most parts of speech: nouns, verbs, adjectives, adverbs, and even one conjunction. Some examples of corpus entries can be found in Tables 1 through 4.

---

[4]While I cannot claim to have performed a systematic search for all possible metaphors, most other work explicitly stating universal claims about the character of metaphor tends to stick to only a small number of semantic domains to illustrate their theory rather than presenting a systematic overview of the validity of the theory over a broad range of metaphors.

[5]Probably mainly through indirect contact via English, for example, *"to call up"* (a computer) uses the same word in German (*aufrufen*) and Japanese (*yobidasu*).

TABLE 1
Polysemic Lexemes

German Word	Japanese Word	Part of Speech	Literal Meaning	Metaphorical Meaning	Metaphor
Haltung	shisei	Noun	Posture	Attitude	"Effect on emotional self is contact with physical self"
Jungfrau	shojo	Noun	No sexual experience	Not used	"Sex is manipulation"
Rahmen	waku	Noun	(Picture) frame	Limit	"Restrictions are boundaries"
abreißen	yaburu	Verb	Tear apart	End	"End is separation"
sich beruhigen	ochitsuku	Verb	Calm down (emotion)	Calm down (wind, volcano)	"Personification"
verletzen	kizutsuku	Verb	Wound	Insult	"Harm is physical injury"
im Griff haben	osaeru	(Verb)	Hold tight	Control	"Control is holding"
fest	shikkari	Adverb	Not loose	Forceful	"Morality is stability"
rund	marui	Adjective	Round (geometrical)	Experienced (character)	"Personality is geometrical"
wahnsinnig	mucha	Adjective	Reckless	Very	"Intensity is madness"
während	nagara	Conjunction	Temporally parallel	Adversative	"Time is space"

129

TABLE 2
Compound Words

German Compound Word	Japanese Compound Word	Part of Speech	Meaning of Compound	Meaning of Constituent Word 1 [Bold]	Meaning of Constituent Word 2 [Underlined], If Applicable	Metaphor (Constituent Word 1)
bodenständig	**ji**mi	Noun	Not outstanding (character)	Soil	—	"Emotional stability is contact with the ground"
Brennpunkt	**shou**ten	Noun	Focus	Burn	Point	"Intense emotions are heat"
Einbildung	souzou	Noun	Imagination	Image	—	Metonymy
leichtsinnig	**karu**-hazumi	Adjective	Careless	Light (weight)	—	"Logic is gravity"
Vorreiter	**saki**gake	Noun	Pioneer	Front	Ride (horse)	"Research is exploration"

TABLE 3
Explicit Comparison

German Phrase	Japanese Phrase	Meaning of Phrase	Meaning of Comparison Word [Bold]	Metaphor
wie ein **Alptraum**	**akumu**-no-you	Horrible	Nightmare	*"Emotions are dreams"*
(fleißig) wie die **Bienen**	**mitsubachi**-no-you (ni kinben)	Very (diligent)	Bee	*"People are animals"*

Classification of Corpus

In most contemporary metaphor studies, data are normally classified according to the semantic domains involved (e.g., *"TIME IS A CONTAINER"* vs. *"TIME IS MONEY"*). Older studies have often used linguistic criteria like word classes or syntactical distribution (cf. *Metzler Lexikon Sprache*, 1993). I order this corpus on the top level, however, according to formal criteria (i.e., the structural construction type and the form of the elements involved in metaphorization) to establish a formal framework for further research in this field. There are four construction types: polysemic words, compound words, comparisons, and idiomatic expressions. In addition, I also indicate the alleged source and target domains for all expression tuples. It is for mere convenience (and with no prior commitment to the cognitive claim) that these domains are presented together and in the familiar writing convention *"TARGET DOMAIN IS SOURCE DOMAIN."*

Similarity Definition

Two expressions are similar if their meanings are equivalent (cf. the definition of dictionary equivalence detailed earlier). However, we do not require all meanings listed in the dictionary for an L1 expression to match all meanings of the corresponding L2 expression. Two corresponding meanings are sufficient. In addition, this definition has to be modified for compound nouns and idioms, which is why I use a definition of similarity according to (partial) isomorphism of the respective metaphorical meaning constructions.[6] Following set theory, (complete) isomorphism between two expressions A (L1) and B (L2) is achieved if and only if

$$(A[a_1, a_2, ..., a_n] = B[b_1, b_2, ..., b_m]) \ \& \ ((a_1 \equiv b_1) \ \& \ (a_2 \equiv b_2) ... \ \& \ (a_n \equiv b_m)); n = m$$

---

[6]Partiality and isomorphism are contradictory in a strict definition; here, two structures that are partially isomorphic have substructures that are (completely) isomorphic.

TABLE 4
Idiomatic Expressions

German Phrase	Japanese Phrase	Figurative Meaning	Meaning of Constituent Word 1 [Bold]	Meaning of Constituent Word 2 [Underlined] (if applicable)	Metaphor
auf den Tisch **hauen** on the desk hit	**tsukue**-*wo* tataku desk-OBJ hit	Protest fervently	Table	Hit	Metonymy
sich **nicht naß** *machen* REFL not wet make	*te-wo* **nurasa-nai** hand-OBJ make_wet-not	Avoid to help somebody	Not wet	—	"Difficulty is water"
das **juckt** *mich nicht* that itches me not	*itaku-mo* **kayuku**-*mo nai* hurt-either itchy-or no	I don't care	(Not) itch	—	"Emotional interest hurts"
eine Wut im	**hara**-*ga*	Be angry	Belly	—	"Emotions are contained in body"

German expression	Japanese expression	Meaning	Source	Source	Conceptual metaphor
Bauch haben a rage in_the belly have	*tatsu* belly-SUBJ stand				
grün hinter den Ohren green behind the cars	*oshiri-ga aoi* backside-SUBJ green	Have no experience	Green	Behind	*"Inexperience is green"*
Ich habe keine 1000 Hände. I have no 1000 hands.	*Te-ga mawara-nai.* hand-SUBJ turn-not	I have no time to do it	Hand	—	*"Help is a hand"*
sich in ein Wagnis stürzen REFL in a venture plunge	kiyomizu-no-butai kara *tobioiru* temple-Kiyomizu-of-platform from plunge	Commence a venture with high risk	Plunge	—	*"Harming is lowering"*
zusammen schlafen together sleep	*isshoni neru* together sleep	Have sex	Together	Sleep	Metonymy
together sleep					

a_i, b_j are ordered elements of the dictionary entry or the graphic form of A and B, respectively, with n and m indicating the number of those elements. The $\equiv$ equivalence is dictionary equivalence. All examples listed in Tables 1 through 4 are related by such partial isomorphism.

Polysemic words.   Metaphor research usually focuses on meaning shifts of words. Polysemic words are the equivalent of this meaning shift for dead metaphors, being words for which dictionaries list more than one distinct meaning.[7] Not coincidentally, dictionaries often mark the first meaning as literal and the second as figurative.

Polysemic expressions in German and Japanese are partially isomorphic if and only if

$$(A[a_1, a_2, ..., a_n] = B[b_1, b_2, ..., b_m]) \ \& \ ((a_1 \equiv b_1) \ \& \ (a_i \equiv b_j)); \ 1 < i \leq n, \ 1 < j \leq m$$

with the word forms A and B being dictionary equivalents, sharing at least two meanings each (a_1, a_i, b_1, b_j) that are identical in both languages, among them the basic meanings a_1 and b_1 (meanings usually listed first in dictionary). For instance, the German *abfärben* and Japanese *someru*, both verbs, share the basic meaning 'to color,' but mean also 'to influence unconsciously.'

Compound words.   The process governing compound words is just a function that combines the standard metaphor meaning shift with a second morpheme (that may sometimes also be a metaphor). Here, the meaning of the compound words must match as well as the meaning of one of the constituent morphemes.
Partial isomorphism between compound words is given if and only if

$$(A[a_1, a_2, ..., a_n] \equiv B[b_1, b_2, ..., b_m]) \ \& \ (a_i \equiv b_j); \ 0 < i \leq n, \ 0 < j \leq m$$

The compound words A and B as well as at least one morpheme contained in each compound word (a_i, b_j; not necessarily the first term) must be dictionary equivalents. For instance, German *Holzkopf* ('wood head') equals *ishi-atama* ('stone-head') in Japanese through the common meaning *pigheaded person*. In addition, the second morpheme in both expressions means 'head.' Although the first morphemes ('wood' and 'stone,' respectively) are not fully equivalent, they are semantically related. The abstract idea of someone not being likely to alter his or her convictions applied to the world of materials demands a material that is not likely to alter its consistence, thus a hard material like wood or stone. It is predictable that

---

[7]Distinct meanings or homophones are clearly separated in dictionaries by numbers or as separate entries.

there is no language metaphorizing this state of mind with a flexible material like rubber or water. These and other compound examples are additional evidence to rule out language contact as the source for similarity: If the Japanese expression had been derived from a German blueprint, all parts of the German expression would in all likelihood have been translated into Japanese.

Comparisons.   Comparisons include an explicit reference to the target domain and a comparison word (hereafter compword) like *like* and *as* in English, and in most cases *wie* (German) and *you* (Japanese).

Comparison expressions are partially isomorphic if and only if

$$(A[(a_1) \text{ compword } a_2] \equiv B[(b_1) \text{ compword } b_2]) \ \& \ (a_2 \equiv b_2)$$

Here, both expressions must refer to the same indicated mental image (a_2, b_2). Comparisons provide the lowest number of metaphors in our corpus, probably because conventional metaphors normally do not have to mention the source domain or the fact that they are metaphors.

Idiomatic expressions.   Idiomatic expressions, together with comparisons, are complex, multiword expressions as opposed to single words like polysemic and compound words. However, similarity of idioms is defined similarly to that of compound nouns: The meaning of the idioms themselves must match, and the meaning of at least one of their constituents must match.

Idiomatic expressions in two languages are partially isomorphic, if and only if

$$(A[a_1, a_2, ..., a_n] \equiv B[b_1, b_2, ..., b_m]) \ \& \ (a_i \equiv b_j); \ 0 < i \leq n, \ 0 < j \leq m$$

Two idiomatic expressions A and B with the same meaning must each contain at least one key word (a_i, b_j) with dictionary equivalence ("light" words such as *the, be,* or *and* do not qualify). In producing the meaning "I don't care," the German *Das juckt mich nicht* ('that itch me not') and Japanese *Itaku-mo kayuku-mo nai* ('Hurt-neither itch-nor not') both use the same key word, *itch.*

EVALUATION

Metaphorization Is a Cognitive Process

This cross-lingual study furnishes strong evidence on the cognitive character of the general process of metaphorization. Although a monolingual perspective cannot furnish evidence for this global claim, a cross-lingual perspective is able to sustain that claim. Metaphor seems to be an independent cognitive force and a central word-formation mechanism that is so strong that similar metaphors can be accounted for in such totally unrelated languages as German and Japanese. I presented a corpus of 106 examples of such similar metaphors in Japanese and German.

Being able to rule out language contact in these cases, it is highly probable that the meaning shift of these 106 expressions is triggered by a common, thus cognitive mechanism. This number may seem small, but is significant enough to point to a cognitive grounding. Furthermore, even if a preconceptual (culturally independent) metaphor is latent in the human mind, its actual realization in a given language may be prevented by many obstacles, (e.g., contextual events; Glucksberg & McGlone, 1999), so that it is rather surprising that as many as 106 metaphors have overcome all obstacles in completely separate linguistic surroundings and survived to become established dictionary entries.

Thus, metaphors that cannot be accounted for are a priori no contradiction to the cognitive claim. Precisely because metaphors are cognitive and not linguistic instruments, they represent simple options that languages may or may not draw on, not compulsory word construction rules. Thus, these findings do not suggest that all words must necessarily acquire figurative meanings by metaphor, but they instead give a nonlinguistic explanation for figurative meanings that are accounted for in two distant languages.

Additional evidence for latent metaphor may come from *possible metaphors*. I limited this research to dead metaphors for verification reasons. If we considered possible metaphors (i.e., all metaphors that speakers of different languages could understand if a foreign metaphorical expression was translated literally into their own language), we would be able to increase the corpus vastly. For instance, German *Berg* and Japanese *yama* are dictionary equivalents with the common literal meaning 'mountain' and common figurative meaning 'much.' Even though dictionaries of English or French do not usually list a figurative reading of mountain/*montagne,* most speakers of English or French would nevertheless understand this word in the metaphorical sense "much."

Tendencies Toward Semantic Domains

Although we have strong evidence for the cognitive character of metaphorization, the formal perspective and the unsystematic collection method do not allow for conclusive statements to be made on the involvement of semantic domains in the metaphor process or a semantic interpretation of the corpus. However, a survey of the involved semantic domains reveals significant tendencies, as a closer look at the source (Table 5) and target domains (Table 6) occurring in the corpus suggests

TABLE 5
Source Domain Areas in Corpus

General Type of Source Domain	Particular Source Domain	Polysemic	Compounds	Comparisons	Idioms	Total
Geometry	Lines Space Size Geometrical Hidden_Objects Boundaries Width	9	2	—	1	12
Man-made objects	Vehicles Money Machine Containers Cloth	5	1	—	3	9
Nature-made objects	Water Landscape Animals Brittle_Objects Plants	5	—	1	6	12
Sensual perception	Sweet Darkness Softness Hearing Seeing Heat Touching	6	5	—	7	18
Cultural abstract notions	Year Admiration Possession Objects Manipulation Forces Achievement Hunting Resource Exploration	8	4	—	1	13
People	People	2	1	—	—	3
Body	Body Holding Heart Injury	5	2	—	2	9
Cognitive activities	Dreams Hurts Madness	2	—	1	2	5
Kinesthetic image schemas	Motion Separation Up Down Close Links Direction Stability Gravity Frequency	16	4	—	5	25
Total		58	19	2	27	106

(the hierarchical clustering of these domains was mostly done in accordance with other studies).

As this study was not targeted at finding certain semantic domain types, it is surprising how many source domains appear to belong to the two areas Lakoff (1987) explicitly predicted for basic experience domains (Table 5). The corpus

TABLE 6
Target Domains in Corpus

General Type of Target Domain	Particular Target Domain	Polysemic	Compounds	Comparisons	Idioms	Total
Human inside	Mind Emotions Euphoric_State Anger Aspects_of_self Lust Thoughts Intensions Health Intelligence Conceit	13	6	1	6	26
Human and outside	Problems Theoretical Debate Possessing Control Intensity Difficulty Interest Harm Understanding Experience	6	3	—	9	18
Human and human (relations)	Acting_Compulsively Contacts Groups Love Personality Influence Help Gaining_Physical_Intimacy Good_Relations Affection Compliance Permission	8	2	—	5	15
Evaluation	Good Illegal Morality Important	6	1	—	1	8
Abstract concepts	Change Causation Time Linear_Scale Force Life Amount End Restriction Ideas Theories	12	5	—	—	17
Physically experiencable	Body People Sex Darkness Things Machines	10	2	1	3	16
(Metonyms)		3	—	—	3	6
Total		58	19	2	27	106

contains 18 such occurrences of perception and 25 of kinesthetic image schemas as source domains.

Not surprisingly, the preferences for source and target domains hardly overlap (if not, we would not need metaphors). The metaphors in this corpus mostly present fundamental aspects of our inner being as a thinking and feeling human in terms of our experience of the outer world (cf. Table 6). It is thus not surprising that concrete objects are mainly found in the source domains, whereas abstract notions abound in the target domain. A joint look at both sources and targets suggests the following tendency: Things that we want to talk about are metaphorized by things that we can talk about.

There are no cultural domains in this corpus. All seemingly culturally biased metaphors were excluded beforehand as they naturally suggest language contact as the source of similarity.

If the source–target combinations found were interpreted as metaphors in a Lakoffian perspective, 56 occurrences would refer to 33 metaphor types as found in works of the Lakoffian framework[8] (Table 7). For metaphors that were not accounted for in our understanding of the Lakoffian work, I established 40 types myself (Table 8), among them metaphors like *"GOOD IS SWEET," "ILLEGAL IS DARKNESS,"* and *"MORALITY IS STABILITY."*

Despite the comparatively small size of the corpus, several metaphors were found more than once. *"MACHINES ARE PEOPLE"* and *"EUPHORIC STATES ARE UP,"* each with three occurrences, may probably be taken as objective, noncircular evidence for real cognitive and language-independent relations between the respective target and source domains, providing the base for figurative readings of concrete words in a given language.

FUTURE WORK

With the semantics-independent similarity definition, a fourfold taxonomy, and general conditions for cross-lingual metaphor research, this study establishes a framework on how future cross-lingual metaphor study could be carried out.

Finally, this work shows that metaphor, like any other subject in linguistics, deserves cross-lingual attention. The fact that English is the metalanguage in metaphor study does not qualify English to be the exclusive object language of this study, which is unfortunately the tendency in much seminal work on metaphor (cf. Lakoff, 1993; Lakoff & Turner, 1989; Turner & Fauconnier, 1998). All monolin-

---

[8]My main point of reference was the interactive Conceptual Metaphor Home Page by Lakoff (http://cogsci.berkeley.edu/).

TABLE 7
Conventional Metaphors Found in Corpus (With Number of Occurrences)

Conventional Metaphor	56 Occurrences
"Causes and effects are linked objects"	1
"Change is motion"	1
"Compliance is adherence"	1
"Control is up"	1
"Difficulty is moving"	3
"Difficulties are containers"	1
"Effect on emotional self is contact with physical self"	1
"Emotions are contained in body"	1
"Emotional stability is contact with the ground"	1
"Emotions are forces"	1
"Euphoric states are up"	3
"Gaining physical intimacy (against resistance) is moving objects"	1
"Harm is physical injury"	3
"Harming is lowering"	1
"Ideas are objects"	1
"Intense emotions are heat"	2
"Logic is gravity"	2
"Lust is heat"	2
"Machines are people"	3
"Mind or mental self is a brittle object"	2
"Moral is up"	2
"More is up"	1
"People are plants"	1
"Personification"	1
"Possessing is holding"	1
"Sex is an achievement"	1
"Research is exploration"	1
"The mind is a machine"	2
"Theories are cloth"	1
"Time is a resource"	1
"Trying to solve a problem is looking for solution in the landscape"	1
"Understanding is seeing; seeing is touching"	3
Metonyms	6

TABLE 8
Other Metaphors Found in Corpus (With Number of Occurrences)

New Metaphor	50 Occurrences
"Affection is possession"	1
"Amount is size"	2
"Bad intentions are hidden objects"	2
"Body is landscape"	1
"Contacts are lines"	2
"Control is holding"	1
"Emotions are dreams"	1
"End is separation"	1
"Force is a stream of water"	1
"Death is down"	1
"Difficult is fluid"	1
"Good is sweet"	2
"Good relation is sharing one body"	1
"Groups are vehicles"	1
"Health is stability"	1
"Help is a hand"	1
"Illegal is darkness"	1
"Important is frequent"	1
"Inexperience is green"	1
"Influence people is hunting"	1
"Intelligence is width"	1
"Intense motions affect the heart"	2
"Intensity is madness"	2
"Interest is body reaction"	1
"Interest is closeness"	1
"Life is a year"	1
"Love is admiration"	1
"Nice personality is softness"	1
"Obeying is hearing"	1
"Morality is stability"	3
"People are animals"	2
"Permission is seeing"	1
"Personality is geometrical"	1
"Problems are animals"	1
"Problems are money"	1
"Restrictions are boundaries"	1
"Sex is manipulation"	1
"Thoughts are water"	1
"Time is space"	2

gual studies risk digging up rather marked phenomena typical of a single language instead of retrieving universal features of the human mind.

REFERENCES

Caramelli, N., & Venturi, G. (1999). The role of imagery and novelty in the comprehension of nominal metaphors. In *Proceedings of the AISB '99 Symposium on Metaphor, Artificial Intelligence, and Cognition* (pp. 87–93). Brighton, England: The Society for the Study of Artificial Intelligence and the Simulation of Behaviour.

Faulstich, A. (1999). Metaphors in comprehension and reading processes: An analysis based on the discussion of the European monetary union in Italian and Portuguese newspaper articles. In *Proceedings of the AISB '99 Symposium on Metaphor, Artificial Intelligence, and Cognition* (pp. 27–34). Brighton, England: The Society for the Study of Artificial Intelligence and the Simulation of Behaviour.

Gibbs, R. W. (1996). Why many concepts are metaphorical. *Cognition, 61,* 309–319.

Glucksberg, S., & McGlone, M. (1999). When love is not a journey: What metaphors mean. *Journal of Pragmatics, 31,* 1541–1558.

Kamei, S., & Wakao, T. (1992). Metonomy: Reassessment, survey of acceptability, and its treatment in a machine translation system. In *Proceedings of the 30th annual meeting of the Association for Computational Linguistics (ACL)* (pp. 309–311). Morristown, NJ: Association for Computational Linguistics.

Kougojiten [Dictionary of classical Japanese]. (1989). Tokyo: Kadokawa Shinpan.

Lakoff, G. (1987). *Women, fire, and dangerous things: What categories reveal about the mind.* Chicago: University of Chicago Press.

Lakoff, G. (1993). The contemporary theory of metaphor. In A. Ortony (Ed.), *Metaphor and thought* (2nd ed., pp. 202–251). Cambridge, England: Cambridge University Press.

Lakoff, G., & Turner, M. (1989). *More than cool reason: A field guide to metaphor.* Chicago: University of Chicago Press.

Liu, L. H.-M., & Su, L. I.-W. (1999). To "run" a marriage: Conceptualization of marriage in current Chinese. In *Proceedings of the AISB '99 Symposium on Metaphor, Artificial Intelligence, and Cognition* (pp. 137–142). Brighton, England: The Society for the Study of Artificial Intelligence and the Simulation of Behaviour.

Metzler Lexikon Sprache [Metzler lexicon of language]. (1993). Stuttgart, Germany: Metzler.

Murphy, G. (1996). On metaphoric representation. *Cognition, 60,* 173–204.

Murphy, G. (1997). Reasons to doubt the present evidence for metaphoric representation. *Cognition, 62,* 99–108.

Neagu, M. (1999). Flowers, vegetables, fruits and weeds: A metaphorical approach. In *Proceedings of the AISB '99 Symposium on Metaphor, Artificial Intelligence, and Cognition* (pp. 118–120). Brighton, England: The Society for the Study of Artificial Intelligence and the Simulation of Behaviour.

Pons Kompaktwörterbuch Englisch-Deutsch/Deutsch-Englisch [Pons compact dictionary English-German/German-English]. (1982). Stuttgart, Germany: Ernst Klett.

Sweetser, E. E. (1990). *From etymology to pragmatics: Metaphorical and cultural aspects of semantic structure.* Cambridge, England: Cambridge University Press.

Turner, M., & Fauconnier, G. (1998). Metaphor, metonymy and binding. Available at http://www.wam.umd.edu/~mturn/WWW/metmet.html

Instructions for Contributors

Metaphor and Symbol is an interdisciplinary journal that publishes theoretical articles, original empirical research, literature and book reviews, and other matters of interest to the broad range of researchers in the field of metaphor.

Contributors should send three copies of their manuscripts to Raymond W. Gibbs, Jr., Editor, *Metaphor and Symbol,* Department of Psychology, University of California–Santa Cruz, Santa Cruz, CA, 95064. Manuscripts should be prepared according to the *Publication Manual of the American Psychological Association, Fourth Edition.* All manuscript copy should be double-spaced. The cover letter should include a complete mailing address for each author and the telephone number and E-mail address of the author to whom editorial correspondence is to be addressed. Figures should be in camera-ready condition.

Contributors are responsible for all statements made in their work and for obtaining permission from copyright owners if they use an illustration, table, or lengthy quote (over 500 words) published elsewhere. Contributors should write to both publisher and author of such material, requesting nonexclusive world rights in all languages for use in the article and all future editions of it.

Manuscripts will be evaluated on the basis of style as well as content. After a manuscript is accepted for publication, authors are asked to provide a computer disk containing the manuscript file. Some minor copyediting may be done, but authors must take responsibility for clarity, conciseness, and felicity of expression.

In order to set off printed *figurative* text from nonfigurative use of (a) italicization (underlining in manuscripts) for indicating emphasis, (b) quotation marks for indicating quotations, and (c) capitalization for indicating headings and subheadings, authors should abide by the following conventions: Any sentence or phrase in which a word or words are intended as figurative should be set in quoted lower-case italics (e.g., *"My soul is an enchanted boat," "to let the cat out of the bag,"* etc.). What are called metaphor themes or metaphor formulas should be set in quoted upper-case italics (e.g., *"LIFE IS A JOURNEY," "LOVE IS INSANITY,"* etc.), with italicization indicated by underlining in the manuscripts. Subordinate instances of these two sample themes should be set in quoted lower-case italics (*"Our relationship has come a long way"* and *"He was madly in love with her,"* respectively). In experimental reports that involve figurative and nonfigurative material or stimulus items, figurative material should be set as indicated above; nonfigurative material (e.g., literal "control" sentences) should be set in unquoted italics (e.g., *This is a literal sentence*).